THE
INNOVATION
STACK

THE
INNOVATION
S T A C K

Building an Unbeatable Business
One Crazy Idea at a Time

Jim McKelvey

PORTFOLIO / PENGUIN

PORTFOLIO / PENGUIN
An imprint of Penguin Random House LLC
penguinrandomhouse.com

Most Portfolio books are available at a discount when purchased in
quantity for sales promotions or corporate use. Special editions, which include
personalized covers, excerpts, and corporate imprints, can be created when
purchased in large quantities. For more information, please call (212) 572-2232
or e-mail specialmarkets@penguinrandomhouse.com. Your local bookstore can
also assist with discounted bulk purchases using the Penguin Random House
corporate Business-to-Business program. For assistance in locating a
participating retailer, e-mail B2B@penguinrandomhouse.com.

Library of Congress Cataloging-in-Publication Data
Names: McKelvey, Jim, author.
Title: The innovation stack : building an unbeatable business
one crazy idea at a time / Jim McKelvey.
Description: New York : Portfolio, 2020. | Includes
bibliographical references and index. |
Identifiers: LCCN 2019046811 (print) | LCCN 2019046812 (ebook) |
ISBN 9780593086735 (hardcover) | ISBN 9780593086742 (ebook)
Subjects: LCSH: Entrepreneurship. | Business enterprises—
Technological innovations.
Classification: LCC HB615 .M3785 2020 (print) | LCC HB615 (ebook) |
DDC 658.4/21—dc23
LC record available at https://lccn.loc.gov/2019046811
LC ebook record available at https://lccn.loc.gov/2019046812

Printed in the United States of America
1 3 5 7 9 10 8 6 4 2

BOOK DESIGN BY TANYA MAIBORODA

Penguin is committed to publishing works of quality and
integrity. In that spirit, we are proud to offer this book to our readers;
however, the story, the experiences, and the words are the author's alone.

To Anna

Contents

Part 3 | *Innovation Physics*

Introduction

S UDDENLY, we won.

For over a year, a giant monster had chased us through the graveyard of corporate corpses. Amazon, the scariest monster on the planet, had copied our product, undercut our price, and was going to eat our brains. Then, without warning, on Halloween in 2015, the monster stopped the attack and handed us a treat.

This treat was better than any bag of candy. Not only did Amazon discontinue its competing product, it also mailed the product's existing customers a little white Square card reader in a smiling cardboard box. Happy Halloween! Was this a trick?

Square, the little company that I cofounded with Jack Dorsey back in 2009, had just done something amazing. The odds of surviving an attack by Amazon would depress a Powerball player, but there we were, still alive after going "nose-to-toe" against the world's most dangerous company. Was this just luck, or had something else happened? I knew what we had done, but I didn't have any idea why it worked. I spent the next three years answering that question, and eventually wrote this book.

This is not the story of Square. Instead, it is the story of how founding Square led me to discover a phenomenon that applies across industries and even time. Square is a good example because I can tell the story firsthand; but if this were just about Square, I would not have written this book.

What happened at Square was no accident; it fit a pattern. It's a pattern that repeats in a shockingly regular manner; and when it does, the companies that harness it become the biggest of their kind in the world. Patterns are funny things, for you can see them your entire life without ever noticing them. But once you finally notice, they appear everywhere. When I learned to notice this pattern, it was like finally seeing the world in three dimensions—I was still looking at the same objects, but now everything had depth. My enhanced vision revealed even more patterns. Patterns that have changed the world.

One of these patterns often appears in businesses whose aim is to *square up*—bring fairness to a previously unfair system. Squaring up can spark a series of interlocking inventions I came to call an *Innovation Stack*, one of the most powerful assets a company can possess.

Innovation Stacks evolve, mostly driven by a survival instinct. If you try to do something truly new, you will encounter a series of new problems. The solution to one problem leads to another problem, sometimes several. This problem-solution-problem chain repeats until you end up with a collection of both independent and interlocking inventions. Or you fail.

We don't see the failed Innovation Stacks because they are never completed; and although the successful ones can be hard to notice, Innovation Stacks are at the core of world-changing businesses throughout history. This book will show you how to see them.

Building an Innovation Stack all begins by choosing to solve a problem that nobody has solved before. Squaring up, righting a wrong, or solving an unsolved problem forces you to be creative even if you don't want to be. That's OK. Oysters don't choose to make pearls.

Square's Innovation Stack helped millions of people make sales and get paid. It fueled such massive growth that our payment volume doubled every other month for three years. It also, amazingly, protected us from a direct assault by Amazon. But Square was not the only company to successfully wield such power.

Innovation Stacks are hard to see in the present. You can view them more easily by looking back in time, for they change the course of history. In fact, much of history is simply a chronicling of ancient Innovation Stacks. From the thousands of examples that illustrate this principle, I have chosen four to examine closely. Square is one of them.

But this book is not just about world-changing companies. I want to introduce you to the people behind these firms, and show you what is extraordinary and ordinary about them. Business stories tend to have too much hubris and heroics, and too little humor and humility. So we're going to meet some famous entrepreneurs, but perhaps not in a way you'd expect. For I also intend with this book to dispel the myth that entrepreneurs are somehow uniquely gifted.

Entrepreneurs are rare, extremely so. But their skill set is not so uncommon, and I believe it to be something you already possess. It comes down to making a single choice: taking on a problem nobody else has ever solved and doing whatever it takes to solve it. The first step is finding a problem that is perfect for you.

There are no checklists in this book. I would love to be able to hand you a map, but maps are for tourists and not explorers. The maps I've drawn from my own explorations won't help you, but an Innovation Stack will. It will protect you from the attacks of massive competition. It will allow you to do things once considered insane or impossible. And, if you dare to build one, it will move us all forward and leave your mark on history.

Let's go.

PART 1

SOLVING A PERFECT PROBLEM

CHAPTER 1

Entrepreneurs and Perfect Problems

BEFORE stalking got such a bad reputation, I was pretty good at it. My target was always the same: some famous businessperson. Entrepreneurship was not taught in school at the time,[1] so I had to invent a way to get instruction. My technique was simple: I would wait until some famous entrepreneur came to St. Louis to give a speech. After the speech I would catch the speaker as he or she left the stage and offer a ride to the airport.[2]

It was a good offer. Ride sharing was twenty years[3] in the future and St. Louis taxis were run by a cabal of incompetent crooks, as if the grandchildren of the Three Stooges had joined organized crime. Cabs would routinely miss pickups or take the scenic route. I got the speakers to their flights

---

[1] It still isn't, but we're getting ahead of ourselves a bit.
[2] With the right attitude and a nice suit, I never got stopped. If anyone questioned my presence, I just told them, "I'm giving the speaker a ride to the airport."
[3] Embarrassingly, St. Louis was the last major city in the country to permit ride sharing.

with a minimum of pine scent, and all they had to do was share some knowledge. My technique worked every time except once.

I learned a lot about business on those rides, but never what I wanted to learn. Every time I asked a question about some significant problem I was confronting, the answer would be a variant of either "You can't do that" or "Find someone who has already done it and work for them for a decade." None of these successful people knew how to do anything that had not already been done. I wanted to meet a different type of person, I just didn't know what to ask for.

The Right Word

The English language currently has no word for our subject, but it used to. Like tattoos, the word *entrepreneur* has lost its shock value through sheer overuse. I no longer recoil when the babysitter has an angry-looking reptile crawling out of his collar or calls himself a "child-care entrepreneur." So-called entrepreneurs are everywhere today, from the local dry cleaner to the freelance designer to the kids selling lemonade on the corner—who, thanks to Square, now take credit cards.

It wasn't always this way. When the word *entrepreneur* first puttered across the Atlantic by steamship in the late nineteenth century, it described a special type of person: a risk taker who reshaped an industry through innovation. Joseph Schumpeter, the economist who popularized its use, described entrepreneurs as revolutionaries and "wild spirits." They were outcasts living on the edge of civilization, doing things that hadn't been done.

But today all businesspeople are considered entrepreneurs, which is like calling all tourists explorers. The problem is not just semantic, because when I talk about entrepreneurship in this book, I mean something very specific.

Let me explain with an analogy. On April 22, 2011, a terrible storm hit my hometown. The wind ripped roofs off people's homes. When I use the word *wind*, you may think you understand what I am describing, but you probably don't. The wind in this storm was oddly selective. It obliterated two adjacent houses, skipped the next seven, and then trashed five more.

Describing a tornado without using the word *wind* is nearly impossible. But as soon as you say *wind*, people immediately assume a bunch of things that aren't true about tornadoes. Wind moves linearly, but tornadoes drop from the sky at random. Wind doesn't suddenly multiply its power, but tornadoes curl back into themselves, becoming strong enough to toss a truck onto a roof or a roof onto a truck. Most places on earth don't get tornadoes, so we lack the words to properly describe them. Imagine the difficulty of trying to explain a tornado to someone living where wind only moves in a straight line. If I say the phrase *strong wind* you don't picture an airborne cow.

Using the terms of business to describe entrepreneurship is like calling a tornado a strong wind. Yes, both the entrepreneur and the businessperson build companies, but businesses are everywhere while entrepreneurship is as rare as a flying cow. The language of business doesn't work when discussing entrepreneurship; the words are already too laden with other meanings.

In this book, when you read the word *entrepreneur*, I want you to think of rebels, explorers, and people driven by more than just profit or even common sense. I want you to experience the nervousness that comes from trying something that might not work. I want you to feel a bit crazy. In fact, a good way to understand the original meaning of the word *entrepreneur* is to substitute the word *crazy*. Calling someone crazy is generally not a compliment, and neither was calling someone an entrepreneur in Schumpeter's day.

Perfect Problems

You'll find more entrepreneurs in twelve-step programs than you will in business school. This may be because recovering addicts study a more relevant curriculum and they use the Serenity Prayer to guide them—*God, grant me the serenity to accept the things I cannot change, the courage to change the things I can, and the wisdom to know the difference.* It's good advice. I've heard similar logic applied to everything from elections to dating. From right-wings to right-swipes, it makes sense to focus on things we can change and accept what we cannot. In fact, this logic is so universal that we can literally apply it to every problem in the world—and then a beautiful thing happens. If you view every problem through the lens of the Serenity Prayer, a small subset of problems comes sharply into focus—those unsolved problems we have the power and courage to solve: they are our *perfect problems.*

A perfect problem has a solution, but not a solution that exists yet. There are countless problems in the world; many of them have existing solutions while others lie beyond our current capabilities. But between these two extremes lie some problems that we can solve if we invent a new way.

Perfect problems need not be massive challenges that affect the world, they can be trivial annoyances. The magic ingredient that makes a problem perfect is *you.*[4] If a particular problem is one that you can solve, then it is a perfect problem *for you.* When future generations solve similar problems they will likely copy your solution.

Will you ever have a perfect problem? You may already. You may have hundreds. But you won't know if a problem is perfect until after you've solved it, and solved it first. The challenge, of course, is knowing what type of problem confronts you: Can the solution be copied? Is no solution possible? Or can a new solution be created?

If you are looking for this book to give you the wisdom to know the difference between a problem you can solve and one that you can't, let me save you the next fifty thousand words: it won't. Happily, there is no way to prove that a problem is

---

[4] By "you" I almost always mean "you and your team." I am going to lean heavily on the ambiguity between second-person singular and plural.

unsolvable.[5] We can, of course, prove that a problem is solvable by solving it. Normally, the smart thing to do is to find someone else who had a similar problem and do what they did. Copying solutions is smart, but it doesn't work for some problems. Copying also doesn't create anything new.

So what about a perfect problem, whose solution by definition lies within our grasp? How do we know a new potential solution will work? Sorry, we can't know that either. We only know that a new solution will work when it actually does work—which isn't very helpful.

The Walled City

This "wisdom to know the difference" is normally gained through repeated failure in a land where nobody else knows either. Draw a giant circle around everything humankind knows, and now leave that circle. I always picture that circle as a physical border, like the wall around an ancient city.

Medieval Edinburgh was such a city, with a giant stone wall protecting and confining the citizens inside. So many people lived within its walls that six-story buildings were separated by narrow streets, called *closes*. Less than a meter wide, closes doubled as sewers and were steeply pitched so their contents could ooze toward the stagnant Nor' Loch. If either you or someone standing above you slipped, you

---

[5] My fellow math geeks may note that there are a few provably unsolvable math problems. But beyond these esoteric equations we cannot prove that something cannot be done. And you are as big a geek for reading this footnote as I am for writing it.

would fall into ankle-deep excrement and then slide down into the loch.[6] The fact that such places became population centers demonstrates how much worse it must have been *outside* the city walls. As literally crappy as life in the city was, it was preferable to the wilderness outside.

But not for everyone. Some people left the city. Maybe they looked over the wall and asked, "What can I do out there?" Perhaps they hated the government, and they walked out. Or maybe the government hated them, and they were banished. Whatever the reason, the people who remained safe behind the wall must have thought those venturing outside were crazy, because it truly was dangerous out there. Beyond the wall there were no laws, except for those of nature. And because nature uses capital punishment to enforce basically everything, the price of failure is steep.

Entrepreneurs and Businesspeople

If you stay within this metaphorical wall, you are a sane businessperson. If you leave the world of the known, you are either an entrepreneur or a corpse. All those people I shuttled to the airport were businesspeople. They were successful and respected; but they were singing the songs, not writing the music.

I might have learned something from the one guy who refused my offer, but I really wanted to speak to his wife,

---

[6] Sometimes when I complain to my wife that I've had a bad day, she asks, "Oh, did you catch the bubonic plague while sliding down a river of shit into an open sewer?" It turns out I've never really had a bad day.

who wasn't in attendance. She was the one who had actually started their business, even though he gave the lectures. My plan should have worked, as he mentioned several times from the stage that he had to leave immediately, and the only other person waiting after his speech was this very attractive lady who seemed uninterested in his business insights. So I was surprised when he refused my offer. I was even more surprised two days later when I saw him surreptitiously departing the conference hotel with that same lady. But then I realized he had a ride.

This happened in 1990, and I had just started a company to build imaging software. As the company grew, I stopped stalking speakers and just courted customers. Anyway, all those airport discussions were not yielding any results. I had no idea back then how rare true entrepreneurs really were.

Let's not repeat my mistake. Let us, if only for the next seventeen chapters, reserve the word *entrepreneur* for a person who does something truly new. It is these crazy entrepreneurs and their perfect problems that bring us the future. I promise we will meet some, but first I want to introduce you to a few friends.

CHAPTER 2

Bob and the Pyramids

I N 1990, my first software company, Mira, began selling document-imaging software. Our product was sort of a precursor to Adobe Acrobat. This meant, of course, that when Adobe released the actual Acrobat a few years later, Mira was roadkill. Luckily, I noticed something ironic at the trade show where Adobe unveiled our demise. At the imaging industry's largest event, thirty thousand people were dragging home bags of brochures on how to have a paperless office.

We immediately pivoted our company from making software to publishing trade show literature on CD-ROMs. Before websites, being on the official trade show CD was the best way to keep your products in the customer's hands all year. And as the only company providing such services, well, *we* were that official CD.

The business grew so fast it was chaos, and not just the fun kind. With several projects proceeding simultaneously there was always the chance of a mistake, and in the spring of 1993 we made a massive one. Somehow we confused the indices for two projects, and two hundred man-hours of work disappeared before anyone could even form the first syllable of their preferred expletive.

We had spent the last two weeks racing to finish this project and now it was gone. I gave the team the bad news along with the hope that if we rushed everything and chartered a plane, we could buy ourselves two extra days. It was theoretically possible to recover, we just needed an army of temps and a way to keep them all awake. I started calling everyone I knew while my colleague John Schraibman made a run to our local drug dealer.

In the days before Ritalin replaced peanuts as the number one children's snack, our favorite way to stay awake was chocolate-covered espresso beans. Marcia Dorsey ran a coffee shop in the neighborhood and was our supplier of this chocolate stimulant. Marcia was friendly and funny and curious about why we were such massive consumers of this particular product. John told her about our little company, about our recent mistake, and that we did things with computers. "My son likes computers," she mused.

John didn't miss a beat. "Hey, would your kid like to make $50 the hard way?"

Meet Jack

Marcia's son arrived sometime that afternoon. I was hunched over a computer with a giant monitor trying not to cause another database error. I vaguely recalled John telling me some boy who worked at the coffee shop was coming over to help. John led our newest employee in and he tapped me on the shoulder.

"Hi, I'm Jack."

"Hi, I'm Jim. Could you wait a moment while I fix something?"

I then turned back around to my monitor and promptly forgot he was standing there. Jack and I differ in our recollection of how long I ignored him, but one of us thinks it was ten minutes and the other thinks it was forty. What I do remember clearly is that when I finally finished and turned around, Jack was standing in the exact same location.

I felt horrible. Here was someone who had come over to help, and I had just been exceptionally rude. To his credit, however, Jack didn't seem upset. I asked if he knew how to use a scanner. He did. We gave him a chair at a brown folding table that had been reinforced with two-by-fours so that it wouldn't collapse under a tsunami of paper. Welcome to the start-up life, kid.

Jack pulled an all-nighter with us on his very first day at work. We sent him home sometime around five a.m. and Marcia was not pleased. On a positive note, pulling that first all-nighter with us made Jack an instant member of our team.

Jack Dorsey joined us full-time for the summer of his junior year in high school and I noticed a distinct pattern in his work: it was excellent. I could give Jack any random project and he would just crush it. I once wandered by his desk and noticed that he had redesigned the company logo just for fun—it was so good it became our new logo. He also liked to program, so we had him work on several software projects. He was shy but brilliant. In a half-teasing, half-praising way I began calling him "Jack the Genius."

Jack was so good that the next summer I had bigger plans for him. Mira's main business was putting scans of product literature on CD-ROMs for trade shows. It was obvious to me that the rapid growth of corporate websites would render our product obsolete within a year or two. Everyone at the company agreed that we needed to change, but I couldn't get anyone to actually do anything differently. They said *yes* with their words, but *no* with their work.

The only person who actually listened to me was my sixteen-year-old intern. I was clearly incapable of managing this company, but seemed to have no problem working with Jack. So I decided that Jack and I would split off from Mira and build the new product without telling anyone. There was no formal announcement; we just started doing the stuff I originally wanted everyone else to do. It was a big project and as I explained all the different facets, Jack began to get concerned.

"Jim, I don't think I can do all that in one summer."

"Oh, I don't expect you to do all the work. I want you to lead the project team. We'll hire other people for the pixel pushing." And so, still in high school, Jack Dorsey became a manager.

I hired three people to work under Jack's direction, all without telling them that their new boss wasn't old enough to vote. On the day they started, Jack waited in the back room while I explained the details of their respective jobs. I told them that they would be working for one of our top people, whom they would meet momentarily. I warned them that Jack was a quiet individual, but not to mistake thoughtfulness for indecision. One of the new hires raised his hand and asked, "What's my job title?"

We didn't use job titles at Mira, but I understood that to many people they are important. After a few moments I said, "OK, your job title is 'assistant to the summer intern.' Oh, and your new boss is sixteen." A month later the same guy came to me and said he now understood why Jack was in charge.

Our project worked, and Mira is still running as I write these words twenty-five years later. After that summer, Jack went off to college, but we kept in touch now and then when he returned to St. Louis to visit his family. I recall sitting outside one day in the Central West End of St. Louis when Jack was telling me about an idea that six years later would become Twitter.

Jack tells people that I was his second boss. Sixteen years later, he would become my first.

Winter Brainstorm

Many things in my town need to be squared up, and these inequalities provide much of my motivation. In 2008, for example, the City of St. Louis dug up the median in the street by my glass studio. Buried below the surface were the old streetcar tracks. St. Louis was at that time the fifth most segregated city in the country, and one of the reasons was that in the 1950s we removed a streetcar system that once connected everyone. When I saw those old streetcar tracks, I immediately thought about a conversation Jack and I had had fourteen years earlier about streetcars. Jack hated the auto industry for the role it had played in segregating our cities and what it had done to streetcars. He swore that he would never own a car.

I had a plan to build electric cars and thought Jack might have some good ideas for me, so I got his number from Marcia. Still carless at thirty, Jack was living in San Francisco, the only major US city that had never removed any form of public transport. He was also running Twitter. We traded a few emails and agreed to meet in St. Louis during Christmastime.

When we met that winter Jack told me a horrible story about how they had recently kicked him out of Twitter. That is Jack's story, and not mine to tell, but for my part I felt like someone had beaten up my younger brother, and I was furious. I even seemed to be much more upset about what had happened to Jack than he was. At one point, I seriously suggested that I could move out to San Francisco and help him get even with a few people. To his credit, Jack suggested that we do something more positive with this energy and form a new company.

At the time, I was mostly out of the technology game and spent my time teaching and working as a glass artist in St. Louis. I had begun blowing glass during college. Though I never intended to become a professional artist, most of my income during Mira's early years came from my glass sales. Jack and I met at my glass studio and talked about what a new company might look like. The only things we knew about this new company were that it would not involve social networking and it would involve mobile phones.

. Jack and I had always enjoyed working together, so I hung up my blowpipe and spent ten days with him in San Francisco brainstorming business ideas. During those ten days we never found an idea that either of us was truly excited about, but we were having fun working together again. Plus, we had already hired our first employee and he was starting in less than a week, so we had to have something for him to do. We decided to produce some sort of journaling app just to get going, and I flew to St. Louis to prepare for a move out west.

Two days later, I was at my glassblowing studio in St. Louis when I got a call from a lady who wanted to buy an orange-yellow, double-twist glass spout for her new bathroom. The chemicals that produce yellow and red glass are notoriously unstable, sometimes resulting in gorgeous hues and other times producing ones like this lady wanted. I enjoy selling my glasswork, but I particularly enjoy selling my ugly glasswork. This piece was definitely the latter and had been sitting on a shelf for several years. Selling it was a wonderful combination of found money and spring-cleaning, like having someone pay to take your recycling.

When it came time for her to pay, however, my customer offered her American Express card. At my studio we accepted only Mastercard and Visa, so I asked if she had either of those. I then learned that the family Visa card belonged to her husband, and he likely shared my opinion of the aesthetic value of an orange-yellow, double-twist glass spout. I lost the sale. Spring-cleaning was suddenly canceled and I was crestfallen.

One of my double-twist glass faucets.

This was just the latest in an endless series of frustrations involving credit cards. There was the expensive equipment, indecipherable contracts, and seemingly random charges. There were so many hoops to jump through that I understood why most small merchants limited their businesses to cash-only transactions.

Still mourning the loss of my spring-cleaning windfall, I looked down at the iPhone in my hand. For an engineer, I have a strange attitude toward technology: I expect it to work. In fact, I expect it to do whatever I want. My iPhone was a magical device that could instantly became a book or TV or map or camera or photo album or jukebox or whatever else I wanted. *So why couldn't this device process credit cards?*

I called Jack, described my problem, and told him that I thought it should be the focus of our new company. I didn't know if anyone else was already working on this, but I sure wanted to. And once Jack heard me out, he wanted to as well. We knew nothing about the world of payments, but we were diving in.

Dirty Money

As we began to learn about credit cards and the way money moves, we discovered a world of staggering complexity. Today, I could give you literally hundreds of examples of how complex and unfair the credit card system was when we started Square. I could explain how that card in your wallet is one of over three hundred different varieties, each with different rates and rules. But for me to reveal how the credit card system actually works would be irresponsible: Any discussion of how transactions are processed would be so dangerously boring that even a paragraph could induce narcoleptic seizure. Add to this the inevitable highway carnage caused by those of you listening to this as an audiobook careening toward the median bathed in sleep-drool. So I have to find another way to convey the idea. Here it is. I promise it will be brief. In fact, I am only going to show you one line of one form from one company.

The figure below is the actual faxed form that I had to complete to close Square's first merchant account, which we had used to test our original prototype.

Merchant Services

> **CLOSE MERCHANT ACCOUNT**
> **REQUEST FORM**
>
> **IMPORTANT - PLEASE READ BEFORE PROCEEDING:**
> ALL INFORMATION LISTED IS REQUIRED AND MUST BE COMPLETED.
> PLEASE FAX THIS REQUEST FORM TO DATA PROCESSING AT (800) 878-6949.
> THIS REQUEST WILL NOT BE EFFECTIVE UNTIL THE REQUIRED DOCUMENTS ARE
> PROVIDED AND APPROVED.
>
> *Thank you for your cooperation.*
>
> Merchant Name: JDJM LLC
> Merchant Number: 4228 9907 0015 9932
>
> Reason for Closure:
>
> ☒ Misunderstanding of Terms on the Merchant Agreement
> ☐ Do Not Need Credit Card Services
> ☐ Out of Business
> ☐ New Business Ownership
> ☐ Chose Different Credit Card Processor
> ☒ Misrepresentation
> ☒ Dislike Merchant Statements
> ☒ Fees too High
> ☐ Poor Service from Merchant Services ⎫ Service was good
> ☐ Poor Service from Sales Representative ⎭
>
> Note: Reason must be checked in order for account to be properly closed. Thank you.

The form used to close Square's first credit card account.

Take a look at the sixth reason for account closure: *misrepresentation*. Doesn't that word have a simpler synonym? The word *misrepresentation* is really just the word *lying* dressed up for a courtroom appearance. Now ask yourself one question: *how bad does an industry have to be before lying is so common that it becomes a check box on a form?*

Confusion and misrepresentation were such a part of the credit card world of 2009 that not even the head of payments for Walmart[7] could tell what any particular transaction cost. The contract at my little glass studio spanned forty-two pages of six-point type, and we didn't even accept Amex. The rules seemed almost designed on purpose to confuse anyone who dared investigate. This was no accident. As I soon found out, complexity hides crime.

Overwhelmed by this complexity, I contacted a friend who specialized in overwhelming complexity as a forensic accountant for a branch of the federal government. Does working for the government, as an accountant, auditing financial statements, sound like the trifecta of boredom? *Au contraire!* Forensic accountants are modern digital detectives with encyclopedic knowledge of criminals, businesses, and criminal businesses. Forensic accountants busted Al Capone. Knowing this, you may be less surprised to learn that the first thing my friend packed for an audit was his gun.

The gun was mostly for show. What my buddy really wanted when investigating someone was data. After he got his hands on the financial records, it was just a matter of time before defense attorneys began saying what an upstanding

---

[7] Mike Cook, who ran Walmart's payments, was the first person to really explain to me how the card payment market actually worked. It was horrifying.

citizen their client was. When I asked him about the credit card industry, his advice was simple and direct: "Only believe half of what people tell you, and always *follow the money.*" Even without the gun, this sounded like good advice.

Follow the money. I began studying credit card transactions and where every cent landed, assisted this time not by a fed, but rather *the* Fed. On page 23 of an otherwise mundane report from the Federal Reserve Bank of Philadelphia, I found the money.

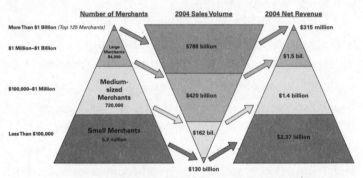

Approximately 90 percent of US merchants process less than $100,000 a year. Yet they make up 42 percent of acquirers' net revenue.

Source: The Nilson Report and First Annapolis Consulting analysis

The Federal Reserve helped me Follow the Money.

It took me several minutes to comprehend what I was seeing, but something was very wrong. The pyramid on the left has merchants who accept credit cards grouped by size. The inverted pyramid in the middle represents the amount of money they process on those credit cards. The pyramid on the right is the net revenue, basically the profits, which the credit card industry makes from all that money moving around. Can you solve the mystery of the pyramids?

A couple of ratios help illuminate the crime scene. Credit card vendors were making 0.04¢ on every dollar ($0.3 billion / $788 billion) they processed from their large merchants. Now compare this to 1.8¢ on the dollar, the profit they were making on small merchants ($2.4 billion / $130 billion). Their profit margin from small businesses was *forty-five times* higher than from billion-dollar corporations. I rechecked my math three times before that number sunk in. Small businesses pay *forty-five times* more than the giants do. We had identified a big problem and a good reason to start a company.

Six months after we began, "the Pyramids," as they had become known at Square, reappeared in the grand finale of our pitch to investors. We set a first-round valuation record using three elements: a minor crime, a confession, and a major crime.

The Minor Crime

Jack and I started the presentation by taking the venture capitalists' money in more ways than they were expecting. After our brief introduction to how messy and ugly the current credit card ecosystem was, we asked each prospective funder in the room to take out a credit card. We had developed a crude but usable card reader and, with this prototype plugged into the headset jack of an iPhone, we read and charged their credit cards, an act that by itself broke more than a dozen regulations. The amount we took varied from $1 to $40, depending on how much we liked the VC in question. Nobody had ever seen anything like this before. Some didn't believe that it would actually work. It did.

The Confession

Having gotten their attention by taking their money, we made our confession with a slide titled "140 Reasons Square Will Fail." The slide listed all the potential fatal problems that our team could imagine, from predictable threats like fraud or bank regulations, to more outlandish possibilities, like a robot uprising. The "140 Reasons" slide was funny, but it had a serious message.

140 Reasons from the original Square pitch deck.

Our "140 Reasons" slide had a miraculous effect on our VC meetings. Most VC pitches are nothing but sunshine and graphs moving up and to the right. To honestly examine all the hundreds of possible events that can kill a new company was just not done. But it showed we were thoroughly thinking through all the angles and unafraid to confront potential problems and future robot overlords. It also had a strangely positive effect on the mood of the meetings.

Normally, the company founders pitch an idea while the VCs try to find problems with that idea. By presenting every possible problem that we could imagine, we changed this "attack and defend" vibe that often dominates such meetings. By the time we got through the 140 reasons, the investors were ready to be led anywhere. We led them to a crime scene in the ancient Egyptian town of Giza.

The Major Crime

The final part of the Square pitch was the Pyramids. We had beautified the original graphics from the Fed, but the data was unchanged. Many tech start-up pitches are awash in mathematical models, sales projections, and other data-heavy figures, but our pitch was remarkably math free. In fact, the Pyramids' numbers were the only market data we presented. We used that 45:1 ratio to demonstrate how reasonable it was to focus on the lowest part of the market: this large, mistreated group of potential customers who were getting hosed by the established processing companies. Our entire presentation pointed to the obvious fact that there were 5.2 million small merchants who desperately needed help, and that *we* were the perfect company to provide it.

The managing partner at the best[8] VC firm on Sand Hill Road said it was the greatest pitch he'd ever seen. We sparked a bidding war that set a valuation record. And yet even as we described our vision of Square's business model and future, we weren't being entirely honest. The truth was that capturing the business of those small merchants was not our focus, because the Pyramids were missing something important: my friend Bob.

Meet Bob

I've known Bob for over twenty years, having worked with him in various glassblowing studios around the Midwest. Bob embodies so many contradictory adjectives that a true description of the man is impossible, so I'll just tell you about his car: a beater 1992 Chevrolet Corsica.

The '92 Corsica embarrassed American industry straight off the assembly line, but only after a decade on salty Midwestern streets does it become a true rolling disaster. Every major system is suspect, each moving part working as reluctantly as prison labor. Occasionally, one of these parts plots its escape. In Bob's case it was the hood latch, which chose to live out its days on the gravel shoulder of some Missouri road rather than spend one more minute in humiliating servitude. After the hood latch escaped, its function was assumed by a little yellow bungee cord Bob strung

---

[8] Yes, one firm was actually better than everyone else, and no, I'm not telling you which one.

between the front wheel wells. The little bungee did what it could, but no bungee is forever.

On the rainy night of March 16, 2007, as Bob was driving across the Mississippi River on his way to our glass studio, the little yellow bungee cord finally snapped. At that moment, several things happened very quickly. First, the wind caught under the hood. Then, that pocket of air flipped the hood up, folding it smoothly over the windshield. Finally, the road disappeared. Bob was driving blind. Most people at this point would pull over. Not Bob. Instead, he leaned out the driver's window in a way that all dog owners would recognize and kept his foot on the gas. But it was raining. Giant drops of water began pelting him in the face, forcing him to pull his head back inside the still-rolling car. So now both General Motors and Mother Nature were telling Bob to pull over. Still, he kept going.

Bob drove seventeen miles that night, in the rain, looking out a four-inch gap between the dashboard and the bottom of the hood. If this adventure bothered him at all, he didn't show it. I didn't even hear what had happened until later that night when he casually asked to borrow some pliers.

So, what do we know about Bob? At the very least, we know *the man doesn't quit*. When the road disappears, he keeps going. Bob is remarkably tenacious. I would say that you would have to shoot Bob to stop him, but someone already tried that and Bob just kept going.

In addition to his superhuman tenacity, another thing you need to know about Bob is that he is also an excellent glassblower. Good glassblowers can earn a lot. I actually used my income from the glass studio to launch my first technology company, and Bob is a better glass artist than I am. Which brings us to the final important detail involving Bob and his car. Despite his superior skills in the studio and his never-quit attitude, from time to time my friend has had to live in the backseat of that 1992 Chevy Corsica.

Why was my friend, who possessed this indomitable spirit and a highly marketable skill, unable to make enough money to vacate the General Motors suite? It took me two years to find the answer. An answer based on the common bond we share as artists: namely, *we sell stuff nobody needs.*

Bob's Car, and the Little Yellow Bungee that Couldn't.

An Invisible Crime

The Pyramids actually showed two crimes. The visible one was the insane unfairness of the system. The invisible, and greater, crime was the millions of small merchants who weren't even allowed to participate in the first place. Bob had been kept out of the market entirely! If Bob could not accept the overwhelmingly dominant form of payment people use for discretionary purchases, what chance did he have? If you can't sell your work, the backseat of a Corsica might as well come standard with sheets and a teddy bear.

On my laptop during those VC pitches I had a photo of Bob's crappy Corsica, with the hood folded over the windshield and the little yellow bungee cord hanging off the front wheel well. But I never showed it to a single investor. Investors like known quantities. If you are asking for millions of dollars of other people's money, it's good to show some hard data. VC pitches that depend on some wildly optimistic projections get shot down—yes, even in Silicon Valley. So during our presentations we talked about what was known—the 45:1 ratio and those 5.2 million small businesses.

Number of Merchants

More Than $1 Billion *(Top 125 Merchants)*

$1 Million–$1 Billion — Large Merchants 84,000

$100,000–$1 Million — Medium-sized Merchants 720,000

Less Than $100,000 — Small Merchants 5.2 million

Totally New Merchants
We don't know how many million merchants

The Pyramid plus Bob.

What Jack and I had in mind looked more like the picture on the previous page, but we never even drew that graphic. Venture capital is for expansion, not exploration. Half the VCs I know won't "venture" more than an hour's drive from Sand Hill Road. I know a dozen companies that have moved to California just so their investors won't have to commute.

VCs fund companies that fit a formula. We fit this formula perfectly, so long as we didn't blow it by talking about the unknown. Funding an expedition into the unknown would require an "adventure capitalist," but they live in a magic palace guarded by unicorns. And as everyone knows: unicorns are extinct.

We didn't tell Bob either. Periods of house arrest notwithstanding, he can be difficult to locate, but that wasn't the reason. I didn't need to find Bob to appoint him Honorary Representative of Frustrated Merchants. I belonged to the group myself, and Bob was our spiritual leader. Whether it was bad credit, fear of technology, no street address, or just being too busy surviving to bother with forty-two pages of small print, whatever kept our members out, we would fix. Jack and I wanted to square up this unknown world of smaller merchants who were excluded from the current system.

We were going to build a massive new base for the Pyramids and shove it under the whole thing.

CHAPTER 3

Squaring Up

WHAT intrigued me most about the Pyramids was not so much the size of the crime, which was massive, but why the crime wasn't even bigger. After all, since serving small businesses was wildly more profitable than serving large ones, why didn't the market expand to include even more tiny victims? For some reason, the pyramid just stopped. I knew that I'd lost that Amex card sale, and I knew Bob could only sell his work for cash, but I didn't know why. Jack and I thought the answer might lie at that point where the market stopped, so this was where we began.

The Market's End

The most interesting part of any market is its end. Why does the market stop at this point? There are lots of customers who would presumably purchase products if they could afford to, but they don't. And there are presumably lots of companies that would love to sell products to these consumers if they could do so profitably. But at some point, the market just ends. This is also the point where entrepreneurship begins.

The end of a market is like a border that nobody is able to cross, a line that separates those who can participate from those who are excluded. Beyond this area is also uncontested ground, which is quite strange. Every other part of a market has cutthroat competition. Any inch of ground abandoned by one company is immediately seized by another. But just past the bottom of a market, prices are so low that nobody fights for this turf. If your backyard is five hundred miles of desert, you don't need a fence.

If you decide to sell new cars for $1,000 each, no existing automaker will compete with you; they will, however, still try to kill you. Experienced companies from the upper part of the market rarely attempt to do business at the very lowest end. You hear such phrases as "We don't compete on price" or "We have a more exclusive clientele." What they're really saying is, "We don't know how to deliver our products efficiently enough to charge that price."

Life is easier when you serve upper parts of the market. If you woke up tomorrow in the handbag business, would you rather have to sell one bag for $10,000 or 10,000 bags for $1? If you sell handbags for a buck, your survival may depend on the price of the nickel used to plate the clasp. At the bottom, brands are irrelevant and command no pricing premium; it's pure market forces. Everyone is free to compete for the very lowest part of the market, but few ever try.

The end of a market represents a standoff between the costs to produce a product or service and what people are willing to pay. In Square's case, this border was defined by about $10,000 of annual sales. Merchants who sold less than this amount were all but excluded from accepting credit cards. If you try to enter a market at the top or middle, there are very powerful companies already in that space that will thwart you. But down at the bottom of a market lies an unguarded economic border. Guards are unnecessary because the rules and practices of the current market make a virtual fence. Who would be so foolish as to try to offer a product below what everyone in the industry knows is possible?

Jack and I were that foolish, and we had found our perfect problem. We wanted to build something more inclusive and fair. We began on Wednesday, February 11, 2009, and had absolutely no idea what we were doing.

Square's First Day

The only things I knew about credit card processing were that I couldn't understand my glass studio's monthly merchant statements, and that my personal credit card would sometimes magically transport itself to some foreign city and immediately begin buying electronics and alcohol.

Square's initial team consisted of three guys and a cat named Zoë in a studio apartment in San Francisco. We divided up the work. Jack coded the server software. Our only employee, Tristan, wrote the iPhone client software. Zoë sat in Tristan's lap to compensate for our lack of health insurance. Since I was the worst programmer of the group (with the exception of the cat), I did everything else.[9] My primary responsibility on that first day was figuring out the credit card business.

It took me only a few hours before I had learned enough to turn to the others and say, "Guys, what we're doing is illegal."

The Moment

In less than half a day we had achieved one of the major milestones of entrepreneurship: the moment when you say, "So *that's* why no one's done this before." This is the entrepreneurial moment when you first realize that you are attempting to do something new and are now outside the walls of the city.

There is always a reason no one has done it, and the reason is rarely that they just aren't as smart as you. As inventive as you might be, there's only an infinitesimal chance that you're the first person to invent whatever you think you invented.[10] There are too many clever people, and there's too much upside to solving unmapped problems, for nobody to have had your idea before you. But that's fine—clearly, nobody has *succeeded*, or the problem wouldn't still exist. In Square's case, the reason no one else had done it was clear to us halfway through the first day, and it became more obvi-

---

[9] This included vacuuming up cat fur and stockpiling lint rollers.
[10] We later found another company that, completely independently from us, was also trying to read credit cards through the headphone jack.

ous over the next few weeks: I eventually found seventeen rules, regulations, and laws that we would be violating with each transaction. This was the border at the bottom of the market.

On top of our growing list of regulatory violations, we had a massive and expanding pile of problems in other areas as well, from hardware to hairballs. Of the dozens of problems we needed to solve, there were five that required solutions that didn't yet exist. Solving these five and the problems that their solutions would create was the invisible force that ended up building our Innovation Stack. I realize that at this point you may have no idea what an Innovation Stack is. Don't worry, neither did we.

1. Software

If you like to imagine the financial system as a collection of modern equipment safely housed in granite buildings, please stop reading and skip to the next section. The truth about how money actually moves is scarier than eating dinner with a health inspector. The software we were building had to connect to the credit card networks, which was normally done through an intermediary known as a *processor*. The processor to which we eventually connected was the second largest in the nation. Its steam-powered computers were so unstable that the firm stopped all new software development every year from Thanksgiving until New Year's for fear that one tiny change could kill Santa Claus. Evidently, much of US commerce still runs on COBOL software that can only be maintained by people who retired during the Reagan administration.[11] Connecting our software with the financial system was like sewing Kevlar to toilet paper.

We had the unenviable choice of connecting to one of two pieces of financial history. One system could process cards securely, but had no way to print the name of the merchant on the customer's credit card statement. The other one was more expensive and less secure, but customers could at least see what they'd purchased.

Every consumer gets a line-item summary of his or her purchases on their monthly statement. The problem was that, under the first system, all those charges would just say *Square*,[12] and not the name of the business that had actually made the charge. If we couldn't change the line-item summary on the card statements, the chargebacks would kill us— we'd be on the hook for any disputed charges, even though we'd already passed the money on to the merchant. So we chose the more expensive option, figuring that as long as we got the customer experience right we could address costs and security later.

In other words, we chose to lose money and take extra risk just to be sure that the user experience was correct. Getting the user experience right was a critical part of Square's Innovation Stack. We were trusting that at some point in the future we would be able to fix the other problems. It is often

---

[11] In 2019, my nonprofit, LaunchCode, is training hundreds of new COBOL programmers while the financial institutions install more wheelchair ramps.
[12] Actually, at that time they would have said *Squirrel*, and I'll tell you why at the end of this chapter.

like this: by solving one problem (the card statement) we caused two others (extra risk and cost). The risk and cost problems would have to wait. In the meantime, we still had to figure out how to read a credit card.

2. Card Reading

In 2009, there were two numbers on a credit card: the sixteen digits printed on the card face, and a secret number encoded on the magnetic stripe. Reading the stripe was far more secure, and therefore companies charged lower rates when the card was swiped through a machine. Jack and I disagreed about which number our system would read. He favored using the iPhone's camera to read the sixteen digits, while I wanted to read the magnetic stripe and get the lower rates. Instead of fighting about it, I flew back to my studio in St. Louis to build a magnetic stripe reader before Jack could build his solution.

Connecting a credit card reader to the iPhone was risky. The only approved way to connect any piece of hardware to an iPhone was through the dock connector.[13] Apple had a lengthy and expensive approval process to use the dock connector, special chipsets you had to use, royalties on each unit, and a bunch of other rules on top of the seventeen from the banking world that we were already breaking. On the other hand, every phone on the market, not just the iPhone, had this simple little microphone jack that was designed to take an audio

---

[13] The official name for that charging port thingy that Apple changes every three years.

signal. In other words, if we could make the data on a credit card appear to be the output of a microphone, we could read the magnetic stripe through the microphone jack. The audio software developer's kit was part of the standard iPhone libraries, which meant that we could write some code without having to ask anyone at Apple for permission. By using the microphone jack to circumvent Apple's dock connector rules, we could have a working prototype in a week.

It's one thing to upset a bunch of banks and governments, but nobody wants to anger Apple. If the Apple folks didn't like you, they just kept your app out of their App Store and watched you die. Blatantly circumventing their hardware licensing process seemed like a good way to get us kicked off the iPhone, so we figured the best thing to do was to get Steve Jobs on our side. Neither Jack nor I knew Steve, but Silicon Valley is a small community and Jack eventually found a way to contact him.

This was 2009 and Steve was very ill, but he agreed to a meeting, which terrified me. Jobs was famous for his obsession with industrial design, and also for throwing things he didn't like at the people who had made them. Jack was going to do the presentation, and I didn't want my partner returning with an imprint of our hardware on his forehead.

To be clear, I love copying other people's good ideas. Copying is nearly always my first move. So, facing a meeting with the most legendary design zealot in modern history, I visited the Apple Store to copy some of Steve's own ideas. I saw brushed aluminum. *Lots* of brushed aluminum. *That's it,* I thought, *Steve likes aluminum!* I bought a block of aluminum and milled our first reader out of solid metal. It took me two all-nighters, but I managed to stuff all the electronics in there. I thought it looked good, but it was also light enough to not injure Jack if Steve disagreed. I showed Jack how to run a card on it, and bingo, it worked!

I handed it over to Jack for him to try, and it didn't work.

I took it back, not quite believing my own eyes. Very carefully, I tried again. No problem. The thing worked.

Jack grabbed it and ran a card. It didn't work.

Our Monty Python skit of "Yes, it works—No, it doesn't" lasted for several minutes until we both had chest pains.

The reader I built for Steve Jobs.

Then I saw what was happening. Because the Square reader plugged into the headphone jack, it had a tendency to twist a bit on its axis as the card slid through. I'd been compensating for this twist by holding the card very firmly but not touching the reader with my hand. Jack's solution was to pinch the reader with his fingers to stabilize it. But our prototype was made of aluminum—and aluminum conducts electricity. When Jack pinched the reader, this created an electrical circuit through his fingers. The electronics were so sensitive that his pulse was interfering with the readings from the credit card. It wasn't a *card* reader so much as it was a *cardiac* reader. By trying to impress Steve Jobs with all that shiny metal, I had accidentally built a heart monitor.[14*]

Sadly, the meeting with Steve Jobs got canceled at the last minute due to Steve's failing health, but it still taught me three lessons. First, be willing to do what is right for the product, even if the industry is not ready for it yet. Using Apple's dock connector would have been slow and expensive, and produced a reader that wouldn't work on other devices. When we made the decision to circumvent Apple's hardware rules, we did it to build a better product even at the cost of potentially killing our company. If this seems obvious in hindsight, the only thing I would note is that no other company ever used the microphone jack like we did— until we did.

Second, sometimes what "shouldn't" work does. Our plan was to circumvent Apple's rules but then impress

---

[14] Because the headset plug could have either three or four conductors depending on whether or not there was a microphone, the grounding conductor was in the third position and the microphone in the fourth. In other words, my aluminum reader was a very low voltage open circuit.

Steve Jobs with an awesome demo and have him save our tails. What happened was different: we built something that barely worked, only to have the demo canceled at the last minute. But getting that meeting with Steve may still have been the thing that saved us, even though it never happened. Apple's top executives were acutely aware of the meetings that Steve had scheduled and simply the fact that we were on his calendar may have been enough endorsement to keep the lawyers off our backs. What's more, even though we were bypassing their dock connector, the people at Apple ended up loving our product. They proved this by later giving us a top-secret present.

Finally, it is important to control every aspect of your product. If we had subcontracted the manufacturing of our readers to some other firm, we could never have recovered as fast as we did from my mistake of using an aluminum casing. Because I had literally built each reader by hand, I was able to correct the problem the next day. If we had been dependent on some byzantine supply chain for our early readers, it could have taken months to correct instead of hours.

The early days of Square's hardware were an exercise in rapid innovation. Our hardware changed every week. I would design and build different readers in response to something I'd learned from the last batch. In most cases, the design changes were necessary to solve a problem, but perhaps the biggest design flaw in the reader was purposefully never corrected, all in a great gamble for attention.

3. Attention, Please!

Humans ignore most of what they smell, see, and hear; it's how our brains cope with a flood of sensory input.[15] But this creates a great problem for entrepreneurs who are trying to get their new thing noticed. Either the new invention is mistaken for what people are familiar with so they ignore it,[16] or it is so alien that people can't understand it so they also ignore it.

At Square, we saw this problem in our earliest demos—even when we showed people our system, they often mistook it for a traditional credit card system. They were equating our totally new system with what they already knew, and ignoring it. Somehow we needed to get their attention. I thought the physical design of the card reader might be part of the solution.

The year before launching Square, I spent a lot of time in Tokyo because the girl of my dreams lived there. On one of my many trips, Anna took me to Loft, a store that sold nothing but phone accessories, and I realized how obsessed people were with their phones. It seemed every person in Tokyo had various charms and baubles hanging from his or her mobile phone. I would see otherwise serious-looking businessmen speaking sternly into their phones while a

---

[15] For a good explanation of selective filtering see https://www.psychologyto day.com/us/blog/brain-babble/201502/is-how-the-brain-filters-out-un important-details.

[16] This is, in fact, the biggest problem we have at LaunchCode. People assume we are a coding boot camp or some other charity that they have seen before. We just need the chance to show them how well it works for their business.

dreadlock of Hello Kitty's friends dangled next to their ears. I wondered if I could make a reader so "cute" that it would have the same appeal as those Japanese cell phone charms at Loft.

Cute meant tiny. After the aluminum Prototype #1 for Steve Jobs, I switched to plastic and became obsessed with the small. Every millimeter that I could squeeze out of the reader was eliminated. This included designing and manufacturing the world's smallest magnetic read-head, which was half the size of the smallest unit on the market. I even lived in Shenzhen, China, with my family for a month to work at the factories that were making the necessary parts.

All this miniaturization had a significant side effect: the card would wobble[17] as the user slid it through the reader and ruin the signal. To eliminate the wobble, I needed to make the reader more than two inches wide, but my cutest prototype was one quarter this size.

I tested the different-sized readers on everyone I could find. The results were odd. If I showed both the small and the large reader to friends and asked them which they preferred, most chose the larger unit because it was easier to use. But sometimes I would not have both units with me, so I would ask a person's opinion about only the one I had. The results were amazingly different. The large unit was interesting, but the tiny unit was breathtaking. People were mesmerized by the tiny unit, but only when it had the stage to

---

[17] This wobble was different from the twist that caused Jack to pinch the reader with his fingers. Our first reader was actually unstable in two dimensions!

itself. It sparked conversations and they would begin asking me all sorts of questions about the company. It was a moment of full attention, a moment of *wow*.

So we had a choice: release a unit that would read everything flawlessly or choose one that at best worked 80 percent of the time but could also double as earrings at the MoMA gift shop. We went cute.

It was a huge risk. If people thought the card reader was defective, they might disregard our whole system. But the results were just the opposite. Our tiny reader sparked conversations. People practiced their swipes until they learned how to get a good read almost every time, and then they would show off their technique to their friends. We had a conversation piece,[18] and the conversation was about Square.

By intentionally sacrificing function for attention we got people to notice that something was happening outside the city walls. But Square could not stay out of civilization forever. We were a payment system that needed to connect to the cards in people's wallets, and these cards were inside the city wall.

4. Moving Money

Storing and sending money is easy if you are a bank. If you are three guys and a cat, it's a different story. Access to the

---

[18] Our iconic white card reader is still the punch line in movies and TV shows. *The Colbert Report*, *Silicon Valley*, and *Curb Your Enthusiasm* have all featured it as a visual joke.

financial networks is guarded better than the cash in the vaults. We needed to find some way to access the banking system, which meant finding a banking partner. Fortunately, there are a lot of banks, and we only had to try four different ones until one agreed to work with us.[19] The card networks were another story. We couldn't shop around—we needed deals with Amex, Visa, and Mastercard,[20] and they all had specific rules against exactly what we were doing.

The card networks' prohibition of our business model was a problem we battled for over a year. Most of that time we spent just trying to get a meeting with someone there who could help. We were able to meet with Amex, but neither Visa nor Mastercard would even speak with us.

The Amex pitch was easy. Jack demonstrated the product and then I gave "the Amex speech." It's what a merchant says to a would-be customer and it goes something like this: "We don't accept American Express at this business because they charge too much, so please give me a Mastercard or Visa." Officially, no merchant is supposed to say such things, but everyone at Amex knew that speech was repeated millions of times across the nation every day. Our pitch was simple. We told the Amex people, "Square will bring you new small merchants. Not only will those merchants accept your cards, but they will also stop giving the Amex speech. Just let us connect to your network." They did.

---

[19] Chase. Those people were absolutely great to work with.
[20] And Discover, but it had a reputation as the most promiscuous network, so we weren't worried.

We had Amex on board within a month, but without both Mastercard and Visa our product was doomed. The problem was that nobody would meet with us. Jack's "Twitter inventor" status could get him some lunch meetings with unhelpful executives interested in hearing about the time Snoop Dogg visited the Twitter office. We had half a dozen polite meetings at Visa, but got nowhere.

We were getting desperate. Our product by this time was fairly refined, but it was still illegal. We tried using Jack's fame: fail. We tried using our banks: fail. We tried using our investors' contacts: fail. We tried hiring a former Mastercard executive as a consultant: fail and a giant bill. Then one day I met a guy named Ryan Gilbert, who had recently built and sold a rent-collection company that connected to Mastercard. With Ryan's help, we finally got a meeting with Ed McLaughlin, a top Mastercard executive, and his senior staff.

Jack and I flew to America's most appropriately named city, Purchase, New York, and entered the white stone headquarters building with our little card reader and our iPhones. Mastercard's headquarters has no soft surfaces in its lobby, just towering clean white stone carved into sharp angles. Jack and I had arrived early, so we had nearly an hour to wander around the massive lobby making ourselves more nervous. We had reason to be, for if Mastercard was against what we were doing, Square was dead.

In theory, Mastercard should love what Square was doing. Bringing more merchants into the credit card ecosystem would greatly benefit all the card networks. On the other hand, Mastercard's operating regulations had language that specifically prevented card-present aggregation[21]—which was exactly what Square did. In other words, people at Mastercard had already imagined a business like ours, decided they did not want it, and wrote a rule prohibiting it. We didn't just have to convince the Mastercard executives to try something new, we had to persuade them to reverse a rule that had been on their books for decades.

After a year of repeatedly showing our prototype, Jack and I could do our demonstration with the coordination of knife jugglers. I knew what he was going to say and he knew what I was going to say. More important, we both knew what the other person was *not* going to say. Jack is very quiet and comfortable with long silences; I'm basically the opposite but have trained myself to never interrupt anyone. Sometimes the key to an explanation is being quiet long enough for the audience to catch up.

Our pitch was nearly perfect. We were so comfortable with our material that we could focus all our energy on reading the reactions of the audience and adjusting as needed. We explained the vision of the company and the reasons we wanted to enable millions of new merchants to accept credit cards. We talked about how Mastercard would benefit directly from Square. Everything was going well until I

---

[21] Card-not-present aggregation was what PayPal did, and it was permitted under certain limited circumstances. But actually reading the card and submitting it on behalf of another merchant was specifically forbidden.

demonstrated our system by charging $1 to Ed McLaughlin's Mastercard. We ran the card through our little reader and asked Ed to sign the screen of my iPhone with his finger. He did, then asked if it was a simulation, and I said, "No, this is live and you will see a dollar charge on your account."

Ed looked sternly at his staff, then turned toward me and said, "You realize what you just did violates our operating regulations?"

"Yes, we know," was my only reply.

Nobody said anything. Jack displayed his normal monk-like calm. I curled my toes and tried to keep breathing. During the ensuing silence I had visions of the floor opening up like in an old James Bond movie, dropping Jack and me into a pool of rabid attorneys. After a full twenty seconds of silence, Ed finally said, "So, I guess we have to change our operating regulations." He then looked again at his staff, nodded, and walked out of the room.

Phew!

And, of course, there was Visa. That was by far the biggest card network. We had been working on the people there for a solid year, but hadn't gotten past a polite lunch date. We might never have been able to convince the Visa executives to change their rules by showing them how Square would help them. But since we'd already gotten American Express, Mastercard, and Discover[22] to accept Square, Visa now had to point its nose back toward the herd. Mastercard and Visa are separate organizations, but they move with the synchroniza-

---

[22] Please refer to footnote 20 about Discover's promiscuity.

tion of samba dancers when it comes to innovation. Visa just does it backwards and in heels.

5. Fraud

Receiving the green light from the four major card networks meant we could finally face the horrible monster that lived far beyond the city wall. The reason the city built the wall in the first place. From the very first days when we told people about our idea, everyone told their horror stories of their encounters with the mighty dragon named Fraud.

Fraud would wait until our systems were running, and then would attack them in a hundred different ways. Each attack would be calibrated to exploit our weaknesses, especially weaknesses that were unknown.

The problem with moving money is that people try to steal it. Smart people try to steal it; dumb people try to steal it; money always tops the list of stuff people want to steal. Every financial company fights fraud, which is a major reason why the transactions are so cumbersome. We wanted to make commerce easy, but every simplification we built for normal people would make it easier for the crooks.[23]

Every person we met from the payments industry warned us about fraud. Two weeks after Square launched its product to the country, I got a call from the CEO of one of the largest payment companies in the world. He took me to

---

[23] We fight this problem daily. We once found an hour-long video tutorial on YouTube about how to defraud Square. I would tell you more about it, but I don't speak Chinese.

dinner at some restaurant in New York City where every entree contained at least one word that I could not pronounce. He downed a martini, ordered another, and then spent the next hour telling me what an idiot I was for trying to allow small merchants to accept credit cards. He explained how people like my friend Bob had bad credit, were unreliable, were difficult to support, and were too small to sue if things went wrong. He told me horror stories about times when existing companies had relaxed their underwriting criteria.

I have a rule against mixing argument with gin, but even without this constraint my rebuttal would have been weak. There was no way to prove that we could handle the fraud because no company had ever provided credit card processing for the people we were serving. From his perspective as the CEO of a company in an established market, those were all legitimate reasons that I might appear to be an idiot. But he overlooked one thing: *we were not building in his market*, we were building a completely new market for ourselves. It is impossible to prove something is impossible.[24]

Preparing to fight fraud is like knowing you have to fight the school bully after school: it wrecks your day, but there isn't much you can do to avoid it. In the case of fraud, there is not much to do until they bring the fight to you. We had prepared mentally for the onslaught, but the actual battle was not what we expected. We were expecting a wave of sophisticated attacks, and some did occur, but the vast majority were

---

[24] Unfortunately, I can't prove this.

from small, clumsy criminals. More important, and almost without exception, each attack fit some pattern. Square's massive transaction volume gave us a great advantage, for it became easy to see these patterns.

Imagine that you are an individual merchant trying to rip off Square. Chances are very good that whatever you try has already been tried by one of our other zillion individual merchants. Being unique is really hard, and this applies just as much to monkey business as to any other business. Even if I tell you, as I just did, that to successfully steal Square's money you have to do something unique, that just puts you in a group of thousands of other people all trying to invent unique attacks.

Because we had such a massive data advantage, and because our users were mostly small individual accounts, the patterns became predictable. If you can predict your adversaries' next move, it is a massive advantage. We created some very unique ways to fight our very unique fraud. In the end, what had been described as a mighty dragon was really just ten thousand rats.

THOSE FIVE PROBLEMS were just the beginning. Solving them created other problems, most of which required new inventions as well. We had no choice. Or rather, we had already made a more basic choice: to serve people who by definition were excluded from the current system. We wanted to square up the whole system, but at the time we still didn't have a name.

Naming the Company

Naming a company is excruciating. A good name should be positive, memorable, pronounceable, and unique. And you don't just need a name, you also need a domain that ends in *.com*. The drive for domains is the reason so many new companies' names look like a spoonful of alphabet soup. We tried all the obvious commerce terms and combinations thereof, such as combining the words *payment* and *happiness* to get *Payness*.[25] See, it's hard.

The naming numbness lasted two weeks. Then one night as my fiancée and I were driving home with Jack, I ran into a convenience store to look for chocolate-covered espresso beans. When I returned to the car, Jack and Anna had named our new company Squirrel. Not bad.

While not the most inspiring animal, squirrels are certainly among the more respectable rodents. We liked the fact that squirrels collected and saved nuts, and decided that our card reader should look like a little acorn. I worked cramming the electronics into an acorn-shaped case while our design team drew images of furry squirrels exchanging nut payments.

A month later, Jack had lunch in the Apple cafeteria and noticed that its point-of-sale system was already called Squirrel. We weren't yet making a full point-of-sale system at the moment, but it was too close to use the name. We investigated other furry critters.

---

[25] I suggested this as a joke, but it got amazing traction among the engineers. Sam Wen, one of our first engineers, now owns Payness.com.

Rats had the right can-do attitude but a bad public image. Rabbits were fast and friendly, but a Google search revealed they already had a contract to endorse a popular vibrator. All the bunnies still worked for Playboy, and weasels were the mascots for the existing card processors. The top furry candidate was the vole, a small and somewhat annoying rodent suggested by one of our small and somewhat annoying investors. After *Vole*, we realized that Zoë the cat might be having too much influence over our choice of names. We decided to explore options beyond simply animals she wanted to eat.

Jack had had similar troubles naming Twitter, which was originally called Twitch in homage to the motion people made when their phones buzzed with a new message. Twitch sounded too much like a neurological disorder, despite the fact that another company successfully claimed that name several years later. His team eventually solved the problem by consulting the dictionary and finding *twitter* on the same page. Jack did the same thing for us, starting with *squirrel* and eventually landing on *square*.

As a noun *square* had a positive and nerdy vibe, but we liked it even more as a verb. To "square up" means to settle a debt or make something fair. It was exactly what we were doing, and Squareup.com became our new identity. We eventually changed the domain to Square.com, but all corporate emails still go to the Squareup.com domain. Squaring up the world of credit cards was our perfect problem.

CHAPTER 4

The Innovation Stack

OUR decision to square up the world of credit cards for merchants who had been excluded meant that we had to leave much of the established market behind. The existing market provided resources only to replicate existing solutions. Within this border, we could copy but not create.

Most people who start a business in a market they don't understand just copy what works. But if copying is impossible, then you are outside the proverbial city wall and the game changes. At this beginning stage, when all options are open and almost nothing is settled, there is a sense of freedom and terror. You face an almost infinite field of possibilities, and no clear criteria for choosing the best path. Copying someone else isn't an option, because no one else has been there before.

As we set about addressing Square's pile of problems, we realized that living outside the wall gave us two primary advantages. The first was that none of the problems we faced could be solved with strategies that existed elsewhere—that is, we couldn't copy our way out of trouble. Either we didn't have the licenses or the resources to employ other companies' solutions, or else those solutions wouldn't work for our purposes. It didn't feel like an advantage at the time. We would have loved applying off-the-shelf solutions to our problems. But we couldn't. We were forced to invent our own answers.

The second benefit of life outside the wall was that we were free to try anything we wanted to. Whatever was possible was permissible. We were so far from the city walls that nobody was even around to ask for permission. *Entrepreneur* is not the only word that has lost its original meaning; another such word is *outlaw*. The modern outlaw is a criminal or lawbreaker, but hundreds of years ago it simply meant someone who had lost the protection of the law. Being outlawed was punitive. People who failed to respect the law themselves were removed from those laws' benefits. Outlawing was often used as a substitute for the death penalty in societies that lacked capital punishment, as it usually produced the same result.

Outside the wall, you are truly an outlaw in the traditional sense of the word. You are neither bound by the rules of a market nor protected by them. What this "freedom" gives you is speed. You must hunt your own dinner, but at least there is no buffet line. Speed is not that great an advantage when compared to being able to carefully copy something that works, but it is one of the few advantages you have, so you had better learn to use it.

Fortunately, being forced to invent our own answers created an environment at Square where new thoughts could germinate and evolve rapidly. If your survival is threatened, creativity dominates conservatism. New ideas were quickly tried and tested.

It was a combination of invention and iteration. These two elements complement each other beautifully. Try something new, see the result, try something new again. This allowed us to solve problems that other companies in the payments industry couldn't. It is a great advantage. As the Silicon Valley cliché says, *fail fast*. Most new ideas fail, or have some glaring defect. Maybe your credit card reader is actually a heart monitor. So build another one. Now.

The Evolution of an Innovation Stack

The problem with solving one problem is that it usually creates a new problem that requires a new solution with its own new problems. This problem-solution-problem chain continues until eventually one of two things happens: either you fail to solve a problem and die, or you succeed in solving all the problems with a collection of both interlocking and independent innovation. This successful collection is what I call an *Innovation Stack*.

But an Innovation Stack is not something you bring home from some management retreat along with the embroidered fleece jacket. An Innovation Stack is not a plan, it is a series of reactions to existential threats. It doesn't matter if these threats are self-inflicted because you chose to leave the city walls or because you were tossed out. You build an Innovation Stack the same way the pioneers traveled without maps.

Square's Innovation Stack

People think the credit card reader that plugged into a headset jack was "the innovation" that built Square. In fact, we never successfully patented that idea, so it was available to everyone. We did, however, have other inventions that made us unique—not that we were trying to be. Whenever we found a problem in the early days, we would look to see how others had solved it, brushed aluminum notwithstanding.

We copied everything we could. Our corporate structure, our legal documents, our HR policies, our location, our cafeteria, and a hundred other things we took right from the playbooks of other successful Silicon Valley firms. We even took some of their employees. Invention was a last resort, and even then, Jack and I never stood at a whiteboard sketching out our grand plan. We did the absolute minimum amount of invention that we could do to survive and, in the process of doing that, ended up with over a dozen things that nobody had ever done.

Jack and I wanted to solve a problem, a problem that was personal for me and the people I knew. Solving that problem forced us into a world where we had to invent. We didn't choose invention, but we chose a problem where invention was the only solution. Our Innovation Stack resulted from our original decision to serve people outside the existing market. We wanted to include Bob.

If you are going to build a credit card system that can accommodate a person who once cut off his ankle bracelet because "it was itchy," you're basically born an outlaw. Once we committed to building a system that was open to folks who had already been rejected by the current market, we were forced down a path of innovation. That path was not linear, but words are a linear medium. So, though I will be describing each element one by one, this is sort of like discussing each ingredient in a stew.

1. **Simplicity.** Jack and I shared a strong bias for clean design. The only thing that I understood about the credit card industry was that I didn't understand it. Even when I dedicated myself full-time to learning how money moved on plastic cards, I was still confused. We wanted to build something normal people could understand. Strangely, our shared belief in this core value was so strong that we never actually discussed it. Discussing simplicity would have been like discussing gravity. I use gravity every moment of every day, but without comment. It was just understood our product must be fair and simple, two values that were conspicuously absent from the credit card world of 2009.

    And so we began with the simplest invention we could imagine: a known price. One price, a percentage of the transaction, for everyone, at all times. No hidden fees. This was exactly the opposite of what everyone else in the credit card industry did. In addition to creating a new level of trust and transparency, our simple price was also simple to explain. Customers knew what we charged, and they could tell others.

To this end, we decided to forgo the per-transaction fee that was charged by all the card networks. This fee was a ridiculous holdover from the time when running a credit card involved actual carbon copies, one of which had to be physically transported to a bank or clearinghouse. Moving three copies of a piece of paper has certain costs that don't vary in proportion to the numbers written on those copies. Paper copies, however, left the credit card world years ago; but the fee didn't. The per-transaction fee no longer had any reason to exist,[26] and we couldn't justify passing it on to our customers. Doing so would perpetuate unnecessary complexity. So we kept our price simple, and a block of our Innovation Stack was set.

This decision had a painful consequence, because we were still paying the per-transaction fee to the card networks. Which meant that on small transactions, we actually lost money. We were forced to recoup these losses by having a massive volume of other transactions. We needed to scale up. Fast. So now we had to create several other blocks in our Innovation Stack to supercharge our growth.

---

[26] Just as this book was being published in 2019, Square rolled out a new US card present rate for Square Point of Sale, changing it from 2.75 percent to 2.6 percent plus 10 cents. Lowering the card present rate in order to add the per-transaction fee keeps the price low for Square customers and still functional in the industry, as we will learn more about in the chapter "Low Not Lowest."

2. **Free Sign-Up.** Our pricing model could only work if we grew rapidly, so to create a fast and frictionless experience, we made sign-up free—another industry first. This allowed millions of merchants who might be curious about Square to give it a try. Free is a magic price: you never have to explain free. Even charging a dollar to sign up would have added unwanted friction, so we removed all the friction by making it free.

   Combining simple *and* free caused our growth to explode, as those were mutually reinforcing—each value multiplied the impact of the other. But many of the people signing up would never become profitable customers, so we were faced with the additional burden of keeping operating costs super low, costs that among other things included a separate piece of hardware.

3. **Cheap Hardware.** In 2009, the cheapest portable credit card reader on the market looked like an orthopedic shoe and cost $950. The original Square reader cost 97¢ to build. Our reader wasn't just cheap. Fifty dollars would have been cheap. It was *ridiculously* cheap. With our costs 979 times cheaper than the alternatives, we were able to just give them away. Even when we sold our readers in retailers like Best Buy and the Apple Store, we would include a processing credit equal to the retail price. Free is a magic price, but it is even more magical if you get a cool piece of hardware for it.

   This was mind-blowing to people who were accustomed to being charged for everything by other credit card companies. In fact, our deal was so good that some people wondered if there was a catch. So we had to prove that there were no strings attached and that they could leave at any time.

4. **No Contracts.** We didn't lock customers into a three-year contract like every other processor; we let them leave any time. People who were curious about Square felt free to sign up, which helped our growth numbers. Equally important was the simplicity that this gave to our system. Since we weren't trying to lock customers into some long-term deal, we didn't have to add any fine print to our user agreement. We built trust with our customers and simultaneously simplified our sign-up. Plus, we never had to fight with anyone who wanted to leave. In fact, in the early days of Square, we rarely spoke to our customers at all.

5. **No Live Support.** We had very minimal customer support options at the beginning. We had no phone number, just an email address where questions were answered by a small team of fast typists. It might sound crazy that people would trust their financial transactions to a company they couldn't call, but few people objected. Then again, if they had objected, they would still have had to let us know by email. Customers who preferred to have a number to call presumably signed up with a traditional credit card processor and then had plenty to complain about.

We took our lack of live customer service very seriously. It was not just a way to keep our costs down, it forced us to develop more innovation to further reduce the need for customers to contact us.

6. **Beautiful Software.** Making our interface elegant and easy was more than just an end in itself. A well-built piece of software paid dividends in several ways. First, it was easy to use, which gave hesitant new users a boost of confidence. Second, it reduced our customer support needs. But there was another benefit that went beyond confident and quiet users: our users became our sales force.

The Square experience, from the hardware to the software to our website, was so beautiful that people started talking. Famous designers contacted us to collaborate with us on projects. We were cool enough that people wanted to associate themselves with our brand. And to keep these relationships strong, we gave everyone a present.

7. **Beautiful Hardware.** It may have cost less than a dollar to manufacture, but the Square reader was a remarkable object. I was obsessed with creating something that people would notice, and even sacrificed some functionality in pursuit of that goal. The reader itself was such a design coup that it has made appearances in both the Smithsonian and the Museum of Modern Art. We then took our 97¢ reader and packaged it in a $2 box.

The effect was like receiving a piece of jewelry. Going beyond what people expected with the hardware further enhanced Square's image as something to notice.

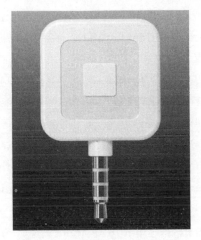

The Square reader displayed at MoMA.

8. **Fast Settlement.** While we were doing everything to speed up our growth, we made things fast for our customers as well. Square broke every speed record in the industry. Traditional credit card processors took several days to pay, which was absurd. This was another holdover from the early 1980s. If you wanted to buy a new pair of bell-bottoms to wear to the Abba concert, the credit card networks had to move the carbon copies around, which took days. But ever since disco died, the only things moving in a credit card sale are some electrons. Yet somehow the banks kept wearing the same powder-blue, double-knit leisure suits. Square

built the fastest settlement in the history of credit cards, faster than we ourselves received payment,[27] in many cases same-day.

Speed was critical for several reasons. It delighted customers and kept our growth humming, but more important, it eliminated all those "Where's my money?" support calls.

9. **Net Settlement.** Our simple pricing allowed us to know what amount to send to the merchant, which we did daily. The rest of the industry had to wait days to know the cost of a charge, and then those charges would be debited monthly. Imagine someone having access to your bank account and being able to withdraw whatever amount of money they think is right without telling you. Imagine trying to balance your books without knowing how much you owe. Eliminating this nonsense further decreased our need for live customer support.

10. **Low Price.** When Square started, most small merchants were paying over 4 percent for their credit card services. News about our price of 2.75 percent spread through the small business community like a cold in a kindergarten class. We never paid a penny for all this promotion. In fact, we didn't pay for any promotion at all.

---

[27] This caused what bankers call a *negative float*. Everyone warned us how dangerous negative float was, but it's not a big deal with interest rates near zero, as they were from 2009 until 2015.

Low price is such a common element in a strong Innovation Stack that we will later spend an entire chapter understanding why. But even without a thorough analysis it is easy to understand how providing a superior product at a lower price enhances word-of-mouth promotion.

11. **No Advertising.** Square grew 10 percent every week for two years without advertising. Our customers told our story, a simple story that anyone could understand and repeat. What ad could be better than a person you know saying, "You need Square," and showing you the world's coolest credit card reader? This saved us money, and it kept our focus on making products that our customers would advertise for us. If your customers are your sales force and your company grows 10 percent a week, then your sales force doubles every other month.

   This growing sales force drove a constantly increasing stream of new people to our door. We did everything we could to turn curious visitors to our website into new customers.

12. **Online Sign Up.** The entire process of becoming a Square merchant could be completed online. There was no paperwork or credit check and the decision was nearly instantaneous. If we wanted to have millions of customers, we couldn't use the traditional forty-page contract. Our online sign-up was so seamless that the same company whose CEO called me an idiot later

copied our user agreement word for word and used it for one of its own short-lived copycat offerings.

But our paperless experience was so foreign to the industry that it spooked the financial companies with whom we needed to connect our systems. So we had to develop a new underwriting model.

13. **New Fraud Modeling.** We have already met the ten thousand rats in the shape of a dragon, and our solution to that problem. Fortunately, our transaction volume was so high that we had a lot of data. This mound of information allowed us to create new ways to fight fraud using data science and game theory.

But many of our customers had thin credit histories, so our financial partners were unwilling to trust them. Even though we could handle the fraud, the banks and processors we worked with were unwilling to give our customers the same access they gave other merchants, so we needed one more element in our Stack.

14. **Balance Sheet Accountability.** Our innovative fraud modeling allowed us to fight fraud better than other companies in the industry, even if the traditional credit card companies failed to understand why. When a normal business signs up for a credit card merchant account, the banks place all the risk on that business. This requires a massive underwriting investigation and a ton of paperwork. By taking that risk on our own balance sheet, Square was able to massively simplify the

sign-up. Putting our balance sheet at risk before our customers' also gave us the freedom to bet on millions of small merchants that the banks would not otherwise trust. We eventually welcomed over two million new merchants onto our balance sheet and into a new base of the credit card pyramid.

ONCE YOU'RE OPERATING outside of the established system, you're not going to be able to survive by just making one or two changes to the traditional business model. Expanding into a market that doesn't exist entails an entire series of changes. Only a few of the blocks listed above would work independently. Most of Square's decisions necessitated the others, and only made sense in relation to the whole.

It's a bit like the Wright brothers and the first airplane. The airplane wasn't one invention, but a whole swath of innovation. Orville and Wilbur didn't just have to figure out how to lift off and fly. First, they needed a lightweight engine with enough horsepower to turn propellers that nobody had built before. Once in the air, how do you steer? No one knew, because no one had successfully been in the air for very long. So they had to figure that out, too. And no one had ever had a reason to develop a way of landing a flying machine either. While the shape of the wing might have been a truly inspired invention, the airplane itself had a massive Innovation Stack.

If the preceding list of Square's fourteen interrelated inventions looks planned and purposeful, that is simply a trick of hindsight. Typing an Innovation Stack into a numbered list makes the process look far more organized than it felt living through it at the moment. Keep in mind, we were not trying to be innovative; we happily copied any preexisting solutions we could find. The only reason those other components of Square's system are not listed above is that they were common practice in the industry.

So often businesses or people try to innovate by making innovation the goal. The resulting "innovation" often looks like bad plastic surgery. At best the innovation is rapidly copied by the rest of the industry and becomes another incremental improvement. I used to start my car by turning a key. Then some fancy cars started using buttons. Now most cars use buttons. But so what?

Necessity mothers invention. You don't plan to innovate, you don't want to innovate, you don't aspire to innovate, you *have to* innovate. It begins by putting yourself in a situation where innovation is the only alternative.

And then hold on for the ride. Your first invention is going to screw something else up. So now you need to—not want to, but *need to*—innovate again. And this cycle repeats. Get ready for a stack of interlocking and evolving inventions, or don't put yourself in a situation where innovation is necessary. Live within the walls and by the rules of others, or get ready to do dozens of things differently. When viewed in hindsight, an Innovation Stack may look like a linear series of wise decisions, but its evolution may simply be a survival instinct.

Could it be possible that some of the most innovative companies were not seeking innovation but survival? Explaining that a world-changing business evolved out of necessity isn't a great story for the history books, but that is often how it happens. Combine extremely harsh conditions with a sufficiently stubborn founding team, and the Innovation Stack evolves. We wanted to expand credit card acceptance to people so far outside the existing system that invention was our primary tool. You don't have a choice: *you have to.*

So We Have To

I heard this phrase, "so we have to," repeated like a cult benediction during the early days of Square. And we meant it.

We want to allow millions of small businesses to accept credit cards for the first time, so we have to *make it easy to sign up.* We need easy sign-up, so we have to *design simple software and eliminate paper contracts. We have millions of people signing up,* so we have to *keep our customer service costs down. We need to keep customer service costs down,* so we have to *have simple pricing, and net settlements, and no hidden fees, and no paper contracts. We need to have a low price,* so we have to *save money on advertising,* so we have to *have an amazing product, and hardware so cool that people talk about it, and a product that they can explain without our help.*

Each new thing affected the other new things, and they evolved in series and in parallel. Parts of our Innovation Stack rendered other parts unnecessary while doubling the importance of still other parts. Everything changed constantly. This is truly difficult, but survival hangs in the balance. *So you have to.*

CHAPTER 5

....

Squaring Off

S *QUARING UP*, which means
to settle a debt, is one word away from *squaring off*, which
means to begin a fight. Both phrases, unfortunately, are relevant for companies outside the wall. Every new enterprise
battles for survival, but entrepreneurial companies face additional threats.

Starvation and Predation

Starvation is generally the first fear that keeps new entrepreneurs up at night: the risk that they will not survive outside the wall sells a lot of Ambien. Without all the city's
support systems, you will just starve to death. Your idea
doesn't work. You can't build your Innovation Stack before
time runs out. You have another idea that might work, but
you are too tired, or scared, or poor, or divorced to try
again. Starvation is cold and lonely.

Starvation may be the first fear that entrepreneurs face,

but it is often not the biggest one. Beating starvation just summons the second demon: predation. Your company has company. Other firms see your success and copy you. They may be bigger and stronger. There may be dozens of tiny copycats. They will try to take what you have built, so that even if you don't starve, you can still perish.

Starvation is opening a coffee shop where nobody drinks coffee. Predation is Starbucks moving in next door.

Hot Dogs and Champagne

Three days after officially launching Square, Jack and I took our girlfriends out for a Valentine's Day dinner in San Francisco. We had a bottle of champagne and celebrated the voyage that had just begun. We knew what we wanted to do, but we had no idea if it would work. So we made a pact to meet one year later, on Valentine's Day of 2010, and celebrate again. If Square was a failure, we would celebrate with hot dogs from a street vendor. If Square was successful, we would have champagne.

I'm glad we made that pact. It is so easy to forget how uncertain it feels at the start of a mapless journey. Street hot dogs and fancy champagne were at opposite ends of a continuum of what might happen to us in the coming year. We had no idea if anyone wanted what we were building, or if we could even build it. We had no idea if Square would starve.

A year later, the corks flew. We were careful not to tempt fate—we poured the champagne into plastic cups and bought some hot dogs from someplace without a health inspection decal. At the one-year mark, things were looking good, but we still were waiting for our public launch. Signs were positive, though, and every year since that first anniversary we have celebrated with champagne. Square was not going to starve.

Customers loved us and there were millions of them. In fact, we were growing quickly. Our Innovation Stack was working—not that we called it that yet—and our payment volume was increasing by an average of 10 percent a week. This continued for almost three years.

During that time the mood at Square was frantic exuberance. The sheer scale of our growth meant that we were hiring as fast as we could, building teams, adding new structures, and celebrating every Friday at a "Town Square" meeting, where everyone saw that week's progress as dollars through the door.

But then there was a knock at that door.

The Perfect Predator

Imagine the perfect killer. From grizzlies to great whites, every ecosystem evolves an alpha predator that can make a meal out of whatever it sees. Economic ecosystems are no different, and it is easy to imagine what the perfect killer might look like.

This would be a firm under the control of a single, determined leader who can make decisions quickly. A firm whose DNA is rooted in technology and the new economy. A firm with nearly infinite money and teams of the best people. A firm that already has a trusted relationship with every person in the country. A firm with a brand that represents value and convenience. A firm with a history of entering whichever markets it wants, and winning.

If you want to ruin the leather seats on a corporate jet, just tell the occupants that Amazon has decided to enter their market. Even a company specializing in uncontrolled bowel movements cannot maintain composure when Amazon arrives; consider the case of a start-up called Diapers.com. Things were going great for the little company until one day Amazon wanted to get its hands into the diaper business.

Amazon cut the price of diapers by 30 percent, wiping away Diapers.com's profits. Amazon then configured the Amazon website to constantly adjust diaper prices to always beat whatever deal Diapers.com offered. Finally, Amazon offered to purchase the company for $100 million *less* than Walmart was willing to pay.[28] Diapers.com is now owned by Amazon. And that's how Amazon behaves when *babies* are involved.

The very words of this paragraph are probably reaching you via Amazon. Amazon has a direct relationship with nearly every consumer in the country, with a treasure trove of data on their buying habits. People pay Amazon to put an actual listening device in their homes. Amazon is literally building an army of flying robots. They stuff the mangled

---

[28] I confirmed this number through three independent sources, none of whom were willing to go on the record.

remains of their competition into smiling cardboard boxes and take over the next market.

And they were coming for us.

A Giant Nostril Outside the Peephole

In the summer of 2014, Square was just over five years old, but since it had taken eighteen months to launch our product, our Innovation Stack was about four. Square was still a simple business: we gave away a cool little white square card reader, charged 2.75 percent for our service, and had a happy collection of small businesses using our product. We were still growing fast. We had no live customer service and barely any advertising budget.

Then the doorbell rang and Jeff Bezos delivered a severed horse head via free two-day shipping. We discovered that Amazon had copied our hardware (albeit as a black rectangle), had undercut our price by 30 percent, and was offering live customer support. Furthermore, it was going to use the ubiquity of its brand and hundreds of millions of established customer relationships to take our market as it had taken hundreds of markets before.

We needed a response, fast. We began looking for examples of other firms that had beaten back Amazon, but if there were any such businesses, we couldn't find them. Nobody had ever written a playbook on how to beat the alpha predator, and even if they had, they would still need to sell it on Amazon. We had to figure out how to respond by ourselves.

Amazon's strategy involved copying much of what Square

offered, combining this with its massive brand and customer base, and then beating us in three areas where it could offer a superior product: the card reader, the customer support, and the cost. Each of these was an area where Square was truly vulnerable.

Amazon's first point of attack I took personally: it released a card reader that worked better than the one I had originally designed. The problem with our reader was its size. The Square readers were so small that credit cards tended to wobble as they went past the read-head, resulting in a misread. Though by 2014 our hardware team had reengineered my original reader several times, they had never changed the size, so the wobble remained. The solution to this problem, which Amazon and everyone else who copied us did, was to double or triple the width.

I had tested and built a wider reader as well, and it solved the problem of wobbling cards, but at a cost: none of the wide designs looked cool. Our reader was not designed to be the easiest reader on the market to use; it was designed to be the coolest thing you ever saw. Our reader was square, and it was Square. It was small and cool and unique. Our reader demanded your attention, first because of its unique look and then because you had to practice using it! There was no way to change the reader to match the function of Amazon's competing product, Register, without sacrificing one of our core values: beautiful design. We adhered to this principle, even without consciously knowing why this was so important. Amazon was offering a reader that required no effort, but provided no joy. We decided not to change our reader design, without ever articulating why, even though Amazon's reader worked better.

Amazon's next assault was on our customer service, or lack thereof. At the time, Square had no live customer service number that you could call. This was not an oversight; we designed our entire ecosystem around *not* providing live customer service. We built our software, sign-up, underwriting, and a dozen other systems with the idea that the customer experience would be so simple that occasional email support would suffice.

When people remarked that it was crazy for a business that handled people's money not to answer the phone, Jack and I would ask them what type of email account they used. My primary link to the world is a Gmail account that I've had more than ten years; Jack has had his even longer. Not once in that time has either of us ever spoken with a Gmail customer support agent. Therefore, it was possible to have millions of happy customers with whom you never spoke.

By 2014, however, Square's product line was becoming more complicated, and we had already planned to add live customer support as an option. But customer support is not something we could implement overnight. To provide a good live customer service experience takes months of planning, hiring, and training, not to mention finding a place for everyone to sit. We weren't going to rush, or rather, we already were rushing but could not increase the pace just because the world's most dangerous company was advertising that it had phone support and we didn't.

Amazon's final point of attack was price. It offered credit

card processing for a rate of 1.95 percent, whereas Square charged 2.75 percent. We could have matched Amazon's price and fought a war of attrition, but we were a small, unprofitable start-up and Amazon was a large, unprofitable household name. Fighting it on price might have driven us into bankruptcy. Our price was not arbitrary: we'd chosen a price that was lower than everyone else's in the market, but also one that if we could keep growing would allow us to eventually become profitable.

Board meetings at Square are usually fun. But the day we discussed Amazon, the mood was as somber as an oncologist's waiting room. Each Square director was given the opportunity to suggest potential countermoves, and after the last idea was considered we reached a remarkable conclusion. In response to an attack from the most deadly company on the planet we would do *nothing*. Precisely nothing.

Matching Amazon's price would just bleed us to death. Amazon would love nothing more than to fight us on price, given that it had billions in the bank and we had only recently weaned ourselves off Jack's credit card. We had already made plans to add live customer support, but couldn't accelerate that process significantly. We liked the way our reader looked and worked. We couldn't match Amazon's size or market share and we didn't own even one flying robot.

By the middle of 2014, we had made literally thousands of decisions about what our company would be. We'd made them with our customers and employees in mind. Making each decision had forced us to make other decisions, so everything was interrelated. We couldn't change one thing and not affect the others. Our Innovation Stack was complete, but we didn't understand the power it gave us. The only way we could respond to Amazon was to change something we were doing, but everything we were doing was done for a good reason. So, we did nothing.

Nose to Toe

Going nose-to-nose and toe-to-toe with a company like Amazon is absurd both as a business tactic and as an analogy. The proper analogy would be nose-to-toe. The size and scale of the massive tech platforms are almost impossible to describe with words, so let me use some numbers. But first, I must stress that the numbers I am about to reveal are absolutely accurate despite the fact that if you have never worked in Silicon Valley you will think otherwise.

In the middle of our "do nothing" battle with Amazon, we were still growing like crazy and hiring many engineers from other Valley companies. One day, we made a job offer to a programmer who had five years of coding experience and worked for one of the other large tech platforms. This programmer was neither a manager nor someone with a rare skill set. In fact, we had recently hired this programmer's former team leader from the same large tech company. This programmer was just a normal, decent Java developer, and our offer was $100,000 in annual salary and another $100,000 in stock vesting over four years. This was before we ever went public, so our stock was not tradable.

This large tech platform made a counteroffer to keep

their employee right where he was: it was *$8 million*. Of course, I couldn't believe this number, so I quietly investigated if it was true or not. It was true. To this day, I have never had the guts to ask why he joined us despite this outlandishly lavish counteroffer because I could never figure a way to discuss the topic without impugning his basic math skills.[29] Not long after this episode, one of my other friends who worked at the same company called to ask if I could arrange an interview at Square. She had absolutely no intention of trading her cushy position for our chaotic start-up, but just the threat that she might was worth millions.

My point is simply this: a start-up fighting any tech giant is like a kid dressed as a soldier fighting an actual soldier. The major tech platforms have advantages in nearly every area that matters: money, talent, customers, brand, lobbying, lawyers, patents, and flying robots. Amazon is arguably the most deadly of the bunch.

Perhaps our response of "doing nothing" in the face of Amazon's attack would better be called "doing nothing different." We were still growing nearly 10 percent every week, which put strains on everything. At that pace, we were overflowing on all sides, from our bandwidth to our bathrooms.

Some of these strains were even physically visible in the form of blue Ethernet cables swinging in tenuous parabolic arcs, despite the fact that we had just built the office we now

---

[29] OK, you know who you are. I'm glad it worked out. But believe me when I say that in 2014 I had no idea Square would become so successful.

occupied—our third new one. But mostly the tension was in the necks and backs of every team member struggling to support dozens of systems that doubled in size every fifty days. Paralleling our customer growth was an ever-increasing assortment of whiskey bottles decorating the otherwise stark white work surfaces. Our cool midcentury modern aesthetic was looking more like a prohibition-era evidence locker.

There was also something odd about the energy in the company during the Amazon attack. The other times my companies were under serious competitive threat, the energy level of the company changed, almost as if the firm had an adrenal gland of its own. I've seen competition either inspire or demoralize a team, but I have never seen a nonreaction like we had at Square. What was remarkable about when Amazon attacked Square was that our energy level didn't change at all.

Everyone knew what was happening, and nobody did anything differently. Of course, during this stage of our growth the energy in the company was already so high that you could reheat leftovers simply by leaving them in a conference room. My view from the boardroom, however, was eerily quiet. We had no idea how well Amazon was doing, for we never saw its numbers. The only thing we saw were our customers and their constantly evolving stream of new problems for us to solve. We knew why we had chosen our path, but we had no idea what would happen or how long the fight would last. We also didn't know how insanely powerful our Innovation Stack would be against competition; we didn't even realize we had one.

The battle between Square and Amazon lasted just over

a year. Strangely, during that whole period, I never saw even one of Amazon's copycat black readers out in the real world. Were we missing something? Were things a bit *too* quiet? But life at Square went on as it always had: we built our products, supported our customers, and kept growing.

Just in time for Halloween in 2015, the doorbell rang again, this time with a treat. Amazon announced that it would discontinue its Register product. To their credit, the people at Amazon were incredibly cool about the way they exited our market. Each of their Register customers received a smiling cardboard box containing a little white Square reader.

I knew what we had done and I knew that it had worked, but it took me three years to learn why. Was this just luck, or had something else happened? What accounted for our continuing success and, perhaps more important, what accounted for Amazon's failure, despite all its advantages?

As I thought about these questions, I began to look for similar examples from other industries, when upstart businesses confronted established companies—even entire industries—and prevailed. If I could find some other companies that had similar experiences, there might be some underlying pattern or deeper lesson.

Something *was* different about Square, but I could not see it. I finally found the answer not by asking what made Square different, but by asking what made virtually everything else the same.

CHAPTER 6

Copies of Copies

OUR victory against Amazon bothered me. Of course, a loss would have bothered me more, but I still never felt that great about winning because I couldn't explain why we won. Without the daily distraction of the battle, I had even more time to drive myself crazy asking, *What in the world just happened?*

Start-ups don't beat Amazon. We must have done something original, or at least exceedingly rare. But what? Nothing we did seemed that unique, and I didn't yet understand Innovation Stacks. I tried to answer that question for a year and got nowhere.

Artists and mathematicians have a clever trick for capturing the essence of a complex object or idea: focus on its opposite. What mathematicians refer to as an *indirect proof* artists call *negative space*, but the idea is the same: focusing on the opposite of your subject is often easier than focusing on the subject itself. Out of sheer frustration I finally stopped seeking originality and began looking for its opposite. It turned out that those answers were all around me. In fact, there were *nothing but* answers around me.

The Answer to Nearly Every Business Problem

But before we explore the abstract world of entrepreneurship and negative spaces, I thought we should do the opposite and discuss the concrete world of business and known formulae. The formula for any successful business book requires, well, a formula. No bullets, no book. No checklist, no check.[30] I realize how disappointing it is to have a book without any checklists. Who wouldn't like to have a map of an unexplored territory?

But this book's subject is the exploration of the unknown; so, as a consolation prize for readers expecting between five and seven bulleted steps to success, I will now tell you the universal formula for success in any existing industry. This formula works from building bridges to selling soap. This formula has worked for millennia and it will give you the ability to succeed in any known field of endeavor. Even better, you have been practicing the fundamental skill it requires since before you were born, and are almost certainly a master.

Ready?

Copy what everyone else does.

---

[30] The folks at one major business publishing house wouldn't even read my draft of this book because there were no checklists.

This formula works even in hypercompetitive industries and is actually not that complicated. Consider, for example, the restaurant industry in New York City. Few markets are more cutthroat than feeding New Yorkers; anything short of awesome is rejected like day-old salad. But if you want to enter the restaurant business, there is a formula for success and people like Randy Garutti,[31] CEO of Shake Shack, know it.

"We didn't invent the hamburger," Randy told me. "In fact, the menu items at our restaurants are all things Danny Meyer[32] ate as a kid in St. Louis. The burgers and fries were inspired by Steak 'n Shake and we got the frozen custard from Ted Drewes." Of course, Shake Shack doesn't do exactly the same thing as the companies that inspired them. Randy and his team work every day to refine and improve whatever they can. On the day I visited him in his test kitchen they were evaluating twenty different recipes for hamburger buns for their international Shacks. When customers have a thousand other options for a burger and fries, Shake Shack obsesses over every detail. "My team and I spend each day working to do everything just a bit better."

But what about all the tables, chairs, napkins, food, cleaners, licenses, and other stuff you need for a restaurant? Randy explains, "Every restaurant in town uses the same suppliers, and if a toilet backs up we all call the same number." In other words, there are entire industries to help you copy what everyone else is doing.

---

[31] Quotes from Randy are from our conversation at Shake Shack's headquarters on December 17, 2018.
[32] Danny is one of America's greatest restaurateurs.

People, especially in hospitality, can make or break a business; but even there, most of all the restaurants fish in the same talent pool. You steal from them, they steal from you. "I just hired the top chef away from one of Danny's other restaurants to run our test kitchen," Randy admitted. "I have to run Shake Shack and attract the best talent, even if it means poaching talent from my boss's other place."

In other words, you don't have to invent a thing. Find a decent location. Hire some good people—whom you should probably steal from other great restaurants. Buy your tables, food, linens, insurance, and all the other stuff from the same dozen suppliers everyone else uses. Price your menu similarly to the competition. Plant a few dozen positive online reviews.[33] Then just work phenomenally hard. (I said it wasn't complicated, but I didn't say it was easy.) If you execute on the basics as well as the average restaurant does, then you'll make approximately the same money a thousand other restaurants in New York City make. Schumpeter and I would call you a successful *businessperson*.

Virtually all businesses work this way. Find an established market and copy what someone else is already doing. Now all you need to do is carve out a bit of the existing market for your new company, maybe add some small improvements that make your operation better: lower price, better product, closer location, faster shipping, or English-speaking customer service.

---

[33] Shake Shack doesn't do this, but "review brushing" is so widespread that, yes, you can even hire companies to plant your fake reviews.

Finding a place in an existing market is like stepping into a crowded elevator: the occupants won't welcome your arrival, but they will adjust and make some room. You don't even need to make eye contact. Want to build an online store for dog food or home brewery supplies? Want to develop a subscription service for accounting software or cheese? Want to mail people clothes in a box every month? There is a formula for each of these businesses. You can even attend conferences where everyone knows the formula. Building a business within a preexisting market is done every day. The test may be difficult, but you can copy the answers from the other students.

Seeing Entrepreneurship in Relief

My frustrated search for originality in Square's fight with Amazon indirectly led to an insight about how to understand entrepreneurship, by studying the force that opposes it. Comprehending what entrepreneurship is *not* can teach us about what it *is*. But does something as esoteric as entrepreneurship even have an opposite?

It does, and understanding the force that opposes entrepreneurship is fascinating not just because it helps us understand true innovation, but also because it may be the most powerful force on earth. In fact, the opposite of entrepreneurship is a fundamental component of life itself.

Every living thing is a copy of something else and can usually copy itself. Every bug, bacterium, and blue whale began as a copy of some similar parent. We may not know

how life began, but we sure know how life continues: replication. We are born from copying and born to copy.

Why? Because it works! Look around you right now. It is
possible, even likely, that everything you see is a copy of
something else. Copying is nature's answer to entropy. If
the world could not replicate successful creatures, there
would be no life. We copy because it is how we survive, and
we are very good at it.

We begin our very lives as copies of our parents' DNA, a
genetic code that was itself replicated millions of times with
only occasional, minuscule changes differentiating us from
our neighbors and pets. You and your pet fish share over 70
percent of the same DNA, and to a statistician you and the
cat are basically twins.[34] Once our cells have replicated successfully enough to be born, the copying just increases. We
spend the first years of our lives in complete copy mode. To
use language as just one example, babies first learn to recog
nize and then replicate the sounds they hear.[35] Baby brains
are designed to copy.[36]

We then formalize copying through a dozen or more
years of school, where a primary objective is to learn the
same things others have already learned. In fact, students
can progress successfully all the way through a master's de-
gree without a single original thought. And even though the

---

[34] See www.genome.gov/11509542/comparative-genomics-fact-sheet.
[35] P. J. Marshall and A. N. Meltzoff (2011). "Neural mirroring systems:
Exploring the EEG mu rhythm in human infancy." *Developmental Cognitive
Neuroscience* 1: 110–23.
[36] J. N. Saby, P. J. Marshall, and A. N. Meltzoff (2012). "Neural correlates of being
imitated: An EEG study in preverbal infants." *Social Neuroscience* 7: 650–61.

PhD dissertation is supposed to be original work, the form of this original work should be copied from other successful dissertations.

And it is not just our academic subjects that we learn to copy in school. We learn to work in groups by copying behaviors from others. Good copying is usually synonymous with good behavior. If you want someone to like you or listen to you, copy what they do. Milton Erickson, perhaps the world's most accomplished psychiatrist and hypnotherapist, went so far as to match his breathing and other bodily functions to the rates of his patients.[37]

Is Teaching Entrepreneurship an Oxymoron?

But *entrepreneurship*, at least as the term is used in this book, is not taught in school. Not that the word isn't taped over the title of many courses, but the curriculum is unchanged. As the tape yellows and peels away, underneath *Entrepreneurship* you will find the *Small Business Basics* syllabus.[38]

My friend Howard Lerner actually tried to teach such a course, and the results were hilarious. Howard had created the first chain of high-end coffee shops in St. Louis years

---

[37] Erickson himself attributed his extraordinary powers to a bout of childhood polio when he was paralyzed and his only entertainment was observing his siblings' behaviors in minute detail. He later learned to use this mimicry to connect with and cure patients other doctors considered beyond hope.

[38] Perhaps with a section on social media marketing thrown in.

before Starbucks came to town. He later sold his company for millions and instead of simply retiring or racing yachts, Howard joined the faculty at Washington University and taught a new class, called So You Wanna Be an Entrepreneur.

"Entrepreneurship can't be taught, at least not by me," Howard told me several years after retiring his dry-erase marker. "Every time I showed the students an example of original thinking, they just copied the example. I kept pointing, but they just stared at my finger." After leaving the university, Howard stayed in touch with his students to see what happened to this eager group of would-be innovators. Ten years later, about 10 percent of Howard's students *had simply copied Howard* and started their own coffee companies. Nearly half the others were working for one of the firms Howard used as subjects in his lectures.

"I guess if I had used baby powder as a classroom example, they would have joined Johnson & Johnson," Howard told me. "The only students who actually started businesses started *my exact business*. It was flattering and insulting at the same time. The only thing more ironic would have been if they had all become teachers of entrepreneurship."

But it's actually good that our schools teach us to copy so well, because copying is the main skill we need in the workforce. From the Craigslist temp to the CEO, the job functions have already been defined by others. If you ever fail to have an answer, you may just be copying the wrong person. Even for the creative professions, almost all the work is done in a synchronized cadence with other creatives. I grew up in a house with olive green shag carpeting, and amazingly, so did most of my friends. We are in such lockstep with our peers that even many independent discoveries happen simultaneously.[39]

We Have Company

How fitting, then, that in English the word *company* means both *a group* and *a business*. These two meanings are closely related: if you want to build a successful business, then you must do what works, which will place you in a group of peers doing similar things. In other words, companies copying companies have company.

"But wait," you think: *"I value originality!"*

Well, so do I. Most of us do. In fact, have you ever heard anyone bragging that they value being unoriginal? Ironically, valuing unoriginality may actually be an original idea. Our peers and advertisers have taught us all to value originality. We express our individuality by purchasing mass-produced products. One of my friends expresses his originality by driving a bright yellow car; but he isn't commuting to work on an elephant.

But don't blame Madison Avenue for the fact that we yearn to be original just like everyone else. The idea of promoting originality has itself been around for ages. Originality is often

---

[39] Calculus, oxygen, magnetism, telephony, and evolution were all multiple discoveries, just to name a few. For more, see R. K. Merton (1961). "Singletons and multiples in scientific discovery: A chapter in the sociology of science." *Proceedings of the American Philosophical Society* 105(5): 470–86.

advertised alongside objects of sexual desire—paradoxically promoting originality by harnessing our primal urge to copy ourselves.

Copying is almost always the best option because things that work are rare. Most arrangements of molecules, music, or managers just don't work. When someone stumbles on a solution, it behooves the rest of us to do the same thing. And so we copy, we copy instinctively, we copy consciously, we copy copiously. Copying is so wired into our brains and institutions that as soon as we stop copying we feel uncomfortable.

Sometimes Discomfort Is Good

There is really only one problem with copying: nothing ever changes. We advance neither as a species nor as a society unless something changes. Of course, most changes will fail. Altering someone's DNA may be the way comic book superheroes obtain their powers, but try that in the real world and you just get cancer.[40]

But we need change. To ensure that our copying doesn't get too perfect, nature requires us to find a partner or pollinator, just to mix things up a bit and maybe move the species forward slightly. To a mathematician, requiring two partners to reproduce makes little sense, and yet nature insists.

---

[40] H. Lodish et al. *Molecular Cell Biology*, 4th ed. Section 12.4, "DNA Damage and Repair and Their Role in Carcinogenesis" (New York: W. H. Freeman, 2002).

Males are basically reproductive overhead. In a few species, largely wolves, songbirds, and humans, the males actually help raise the young,[41] but most males don't. Males are simply a parking space for DNA. Do the math: with four asexual adults (females) you get eight offspring, but with two males and two females you get only four offspring (remember, most males don't help raise, and some will occasionally eat, the kids). So, the asexually reproducing population grows twice as fast as the sexual one. Math hates men.

But look out the window and you will see that almost all species use sexual reproduction. Why? Because perfect copies lose out over time. Without the ability to adapt, asexual species evolve more slowly and are less able to handle a changing world, so the sexual reproducers win, even if it means tolerating men. This has been proven in both the laboratory and the natural world.[42] It is also true in business. Companies constantly strive to improve their products or processes in a manner similar to natural evolution.

So both Mother Nature and Mister Market want change. Normally this change is slow, but not always. Occasionally a species or a company finds itself in an ecosystem with no natural competitors, and then the growth can be explosive. But while invasive species are generally bad, invasive companies can be good.

---

[41] As I write this, I am watching one of my own little copies teething on an electrical cord.

[42] J. F. Crow (1994). "Advantages of sexual reproduction." *Developmental Genetics* 15(3): 205–13. www.ncbi.nlm.nih.gov/pubmed/8062455.

Unlike the physical world, which has a limited amount of area, the realm of business is infinite. Creating new markets is not zero-sum. The invention of the airplane did not cause the demise of the automobile. And while species compete for sunlight and protein, in the world of business you can grow without destroying your neighbor. In fact, the history of humanity has seen nearly continuous economic growth.[43] Most of this growth is steady, incremental progress. Cell phones used to be slow and unreliable; now they are fast and unreliable. But occasionally there are breakthroughs that bring explosive growth, like the first cell phone system.

Copying and innovation are partners. If you choose to solve a perfect problem and create explosive growth, most of what you do will still be copying, you just won't copy *everything*. Copy when you can; invent when you must.

Copying is a great thing, but it should not be our only thing. Copying is almost always the way to counter a competitor, but it will never produce a situation where no competitors exist. Copying almost always feels comfortable, but it will never produce the thrill of invention. Copying is almost always the right answer, but it will never produce transformative change.

Of course, if you never do anything but copy, society will embrace you. Conversely, if you reject the proven way,

---

[43] L. Neal and R. Cameron. *A Concise Economic History of the World* (New York: Oxford, 2003).

society may reject you. The odds of succeeding as a businessperson dwarf those of succeeding as an entrepreneur. Given these risks, it may seem crazy to become an entrepreneur. But some of us do.

Why?

PART 2

THE MYTHICAL EXPERT

YOU CAN HAVE a great life copying other people who have great lives. Copying is such a supremely powerful tool that it begs the question: why would someone choose to do anything else? Given the safety and predictability of copying and making incremental improvements, why risk total failure by taking a transformative leap? But some do choose to leave that walled city. Are they crazy? What is their motivation?

For those who choose to leave, two types of motivation matter. The first type is the motivation we all know—let's call this *perseverance*. Perseverance powers us to finish tasks, to get going and keep going. There are entire industries dedicated to perseverance. You can attend weeklong seminars to improve your perseverance. It is the key to success in most endeavors. We also call it *work ethic, follow-through, grit, determination*, or some other universally respected term.

The second type of motivation, however, applies only to entrepreneurs and artists and is rarely discussed—let's call this *audacity*. Audacity is the reason you decide to leave the city and attempt something that has never been done. Audacity is generally frowned upon, or at best respected in hindsight if and when you succeed. We have no glowing nouns for people who reject our trusted ways.

Once you have the audacity to walk out of the walled city and try something entirely new, you shouldn't have any problem with perseverance. If you quit, you die. Seminar over. Fear fuels your survival instinct, and you will leap from invention to invention that necessity will mother. The "decision" to innovate is easy to make, as there is little choice.

You don't choose to do a dozen things to survive, you just choose to survive—and are forced to do a dozen things. So the real choice, then, is about whether to tackle a perfect problem or not. Ultimately, the decision to do something new comes down to a battle between the audacity you have to solve a perfect problem and your fear of failure. How much do you care versus how much does it cost. If you care enough, failure be damned.

These high stakes make this initial decision to leave the city even more difficult. Audacity is a deeply personal subject and very hard to understand. I've studied entrepreneurs in writing and in person, but I can only guess at their motivations. Better to just share their stories and let you guess for yourself. The question remains the same: *why did you leave the safety of the walled city?* Everyone in the city thinks leaving is crazy.

But to comprehend crazy, you must actually know someone's mind, which may be the reason we never hear discussions of audacity. It would be great to understand the motivation behind seemingly crazy behavior, but how? The driving force behind entrepreneurship is so personal, it is nearly impossible to study.

In place of studies, I offer stories. I want you to meet some entrepreneurs and hear what happened to them. I want you to have your own insights into audacity. Beginning with a seven-year-old boy I knew well.

CHAPTER 7

Lemonade

MY first real business transaction was at a cash-only lemonade stand in my neighborhood. It was three years after men first landed on the moon, so instead of lemonade, orange Tang was the drink for sale. Sweet, powdered science! Nothing could be better on a hot St. Louis afternoon. I paid my dime and got my cup, but something was wrong with my Tang. The boys running the stand thought it would be fun to dilute my drink with so much water that it didn't even turn my tongue orange. I complained, but they insisted that the contents of my Dixie cup met NASA standards.

They made me drink the remains of the other kids' cups to prove their case, all the while laughing and maintaining that they had done nothing wrong. Consumer protection in 1972 was directly proportional to one's ability to fight, and being a skinny seven-year-old without an older sibling, my best option was to let them take my money. I remember that feeling of being so powerless I could not even express my anger. It took every bit of strength I had to keep from crying until I could get away.

Anger is a crazy energy source, like a tank of gasoline. Once considered too dangerous and explosive to be anything but industrial waste,[44] gasoline now powers us around the planet. Giant explosion or a trip to Wisconsin, it all depends on how you use it. The thermodynamics of anger management were taught by example in my family. My father, a chemical engineering professor and dean of Washington University's engineering school, never once lost his temper. In fifty years I heard the man swear precisely twice. I learned from birth not to smoke while filling up the tank.

That lemonade stand was my first memory of being angry and powerless. I never had the guts or wits to do anything to those boys, which is probably why the memory is still so strong. Being teased and picked on was normal for my friends and me; the hard part was not letting the bullies see you cry. I reinforced my gas tank, strengthening it over the years to contain an explosion that would otherwise level a city block. By the time I entered college, my tank was ready for another test, and I actually had a response this time. A crazy response.

Of course, crazy is a matter of opinion. You can do something that appears crazy for a very rational reason.

---

[44] Gasoline was the unwanted by-product of refining kerosene. While kerosene went to work lighting the homes of America, its bipolar hydrocarbon cousin was dumped onto the ground and poured into rivers. The Cuyahoga River in Ohio used to regularly catch fire.

You can also do something that appears rational for a crazy reason. Like writing a textbook. I have now written three textbooks, two on computer programming and one on glassblowing, but my first book was crazy. Nothing appears at first glance to be more rational than a textbook on computer programming: it's basically a bunch of logical statements, in a logical order, explained logically. Computer textbooks have no characters or plot. But they can still be nuts.

I wrote my first textbook when I was eighteen years old, driven by a full tank of anger. It was the fall of 1983, and I was a freshman studying economics at Washington University. I had no interest in computers, though one might conclude otherwise by the way I dressed. Nobody had sent me the memo that boldly striped, knee-length tube socks had gone out of fashion. I still wore the blue jeans that my mom had purchased when I was much shorter and then hemmed out as I grew, leaving annual growth rings around my ankles. Finally, to ensure that my shirts would cover my freakishly long arms, I purchased them several sizes too large for my body, making me look like a scarecrow that had lost its straw. But despite meeting the dress code, I was never a member of the computer club.

But the machines were coming, and the windowless computer lab at Washington University's engineering school had this cool Mission Control vibe from all the green monitors. I took a CS-135 class and then CS-236. "Two thirty-six," as we called it, required the purchase of a $45 textbook, which not coincidentally was written by the chairman of the computer science department. I was proud to be attending a school with a faculty so accomplished that they wrote our textbooks.

I still remember that book, with its stiff hardback cover that made it snap shut like an alligator's jaw if I tried to read it while typing at the computer. Little did I realize that the overly aggressive binding was simply the publisher's effort to protect students from the book's contents. Once I learned to wedge the book open by jamming it under the desk with my knee as I typed, the trouble really began. The book read like a piece of tax legislation, but more troubling was the fact that *none* of the programming examples worked. Some of the sample programs were simply wrong, but even the ones that weren't riddled with errors still didn't work since they were written in PL/1, an archaic language that no computer on campus could run.

The only thing about that book that functioned properly was the 15 percent royalty payment the author received on each copy. Students were being forced to purchase an outdated, poorly written, overpriced book so the CS chairman could make a few bucks off us. I was so mad I could taste the watered-down Tang. But this time, instead of running home and crying, I decided to write a new textbook so that future students could avoid my frustration.

Both my motivation and my goal were crazy. Writing a textbook out of spite was odd enough, but way worse was a total lack of knowledge about my book's subject. I'd never programmed a computer before college and was not even enrolled in the engineering school. I had neither qualification as a writer nor experience or interest in the subject. Writing textbooks was just not something students, let alone freshman students, did. To make matters worse, I openly admitted that my motivation for this irrational journey was to correct the mistake of the person who would be giving me grades for the next several years.

I wrote it anyway. With the help of friends, teachers, and a summer in the library, the book came together. I knew exactly what I wanted, since I was still a student and painfully aware of how difficult some of the lessons were. By the start of my sophomore year, I had produced a book that was exactly what I would have wanted as a freshman CS student. Perhaps because the book was quite different from "normal" textbooks at the time, it caught the attention of both Prentice Hall and Wadsworth, the nation's top textbook publishing houses. The senior editor at Wadsworth called my father's office and said, "Professor McKelvey, we would like to publish your book." Dad realized what had happened and calmly replied, "I think you want a different Professor McKelvey."

The book was good enough to become the course text for CS-236, and Wadsworth subsequently asked me to write another one. My second book briefly became a bestseller.[45] Word spread around campus about how this freshman kid had written a textbook, and I acquired a completely undeserved reputation as someone who knew computers. It was

---

[45] This was mostly lucky timing. They calculate sales statistics by sampling orders and my book had just had a great month.

my first lesson on how commitment can substitute for qualification.

Was writing my first book crazy? Certainly the people who watched me do it thought so. I was too busy researching and writing to pay much attention, but I don't deny that the word fits. I'm OK with people thinking my objectives or motivations are crazy, or at least I've become desensitized to the label.

I've undertaken a dozen projects that people have called crazy. I've made a living as an artist and started a glassblowing studio. I've founded companies in the fields of software, book printing, roofing, and payments. I launched a nonprofit to solve the national shortage of programmers. I'm currently trying to give people control of their online identities. I have no idea what, if anything, these organizations have in common except that at the core is a problem that I care about.

Caring about something is an audacious source of energy. The problem could be a murder, a hurricane, a suicide, fake news, or something else. And though I no longer feel motivated by anger, I will admit that there is still some of that seven-year-old boy who comes to work with me every day.

CHAPTER 8

Entrepreneurs Everywhere

AFTER Square survived the Amazon attack I wanted to meet other survivors, trade stories, and maybe make some T-shirts. But I couldn't find any other survivors. I did locate several people who had lost their companies to Amazon, and asked to interview them for this book, but they all refused to say anything on the record. Even after the fight ended, nobody would talk about it. Try as I might, I've never been able to meet the minimum T-shirt order.

Having peers would be great, but what I have always really wanted was a big brother or a mentor: someone who had walked my path before me. Unfortunately, the number of glassblowing engineer-economists is a very small club, despite our loose dress code. I am fortunate to have a father who taught me how to find patterns, if not patrons. Was there anything in the data that implied a larger truth?

But Dad was a scientist, and much of his advice didn't work for me outside the lab—or outside the proverbial wall.

Whenever some oddball calamity had my palms sweating, I always asked myself what my father would do in this situation. The answer was always the same: *Dad would not be in this situation!* I eventually quit looking for a mentor and just tried to develop a sense of humor.

I learned most of my survival skills from my mother, an extroverted and fearless New Yorker. She died before I learned to fully disregard what other people thought, but she taught me audacity. One day in high school, I was watching TV with a girlfriend whom my mother described as "decorative." Mom came into the room to say something and saw a cockroach climbing one of her curtains. Without even pausing, Mom grabbed the bug in her bare hand while she finished conversing with this girl. The captive cockroach and my distressed date then began a squirming contest, each one regretting their encounter with Edith McKelvey. Neither visited our house again. My mother would never tell me whom to date, but she had no problem scaring away the ones she didn't like. Mom was queen of the unusual solution.

But ultimately neither of my parents understood my path. Nobody did, including me. If I could ever find a mentor, I had my first question ready to go: *did they have a formula?* Could success be replicated, or even recognized? Even my successes seemed random. I could never find a pattern in the data. Maybe it was just luck.

People don't give luck enough credit. Try this thought experiment: Let's define success as flipping heads ten coin tosses in a row. Imagine a thousand people in the same room trying to do it. The chance of someone succeeding is the reciprocal of 2^{10}, or one out of 1,024, so there's probably someone who will succeed. But picture how this happens in the room. After six flips, most everyone will have flipped tails and been eliminated. So they now start crowding around the few people still going—after seven flips, there will be about eight of them left—and trying to determine how these people do it. Those still flipping coins will be concentrating hard on getting heads to come up again to stay in the contest. After the eighth flip, we should be down to about four remaining in the game, and the people crowding around them will be asking, "What's your secret?" After the ninth flip, statistically we should be down to two, and maybe one of them explains: "Oh, I dry my hands after every flip and visualize heads." The other person says she lowers her hand very slowly before flipping the coin, and that that's always worked for her.

Luck never *feels* like luck if you were working hard when you happened to get lucky. Successful people like to credit their diligence or intelligence, but maybe they just flipped heads ten times in succession. I thought something we did at Square might reveal a more general lesson or something that could even be replicated. But with no mentor to query and no other examples to examine, I was just another guy drying his hands and visualizing heads.

---

[10] This is not a footnote; that's 2 to the 10th power.

Spanish Venture Capital

Then one day I went to a party in a palace. The palace owners were an old and formerly wealthy family, but any modicum of enterprise had been bred[46] out over the centuries. Now their main source of income was renting out their ancestral home like some aristocratic Airbnb. The extent of their risk tolerance these days was to permit red wine, which is evidently a big deal when the carpet is historically significant. But, as a display in their library made clear, this had once been a family of venture capitalists. In fact, as I examined their ancestral artifacts I learned that they had supported one of the most daring ventures in history.

Preserved and on display in that library were original letters from Christopher Columbus, in which the future Admiral of the Ocean Sea sought money from this family for his outrageous plan: to reach India by sailing west across the Atlantic. And these people wrote back! They were some of his funders, and I was awestruck. As I looked at these letters, I was amazed at what it must have taken for Columbus to even propose this. I was viewing Columbus's pitch deck. And it wasn't an easy pitch.

European kingdoms needed a new route to the Indies. The Ottoman navy had a strongly defended line in the Mediterranean that kept Europe's access to eastern trade routes limited. A new commercial route would be immensely valuable, and yet King John II of Portugal, whom Columbus

---

[46] Well, this was European royalty, so perhaps inbred.

pitched first, had no interest in supplying the venture. Queen Isabella of Castile hemmed and hawed for six years. So, given the massive value, people must have had serious doubts that what he wanted to do was possible.

Yet Columbus was doggedly determined to do this crazy thing. People used to say that he proved the world wasn't flat. We know better than that now. Navigators at that time certainly knew the world was round. What they didn't know was how big it was. Columbus really had no idea how long it would take to sail to where he thought he was going, or what he would ultimately find there. How do you plan for a trip like that? How do you pack? How do you convince sailors, who presumably value their lives, to join?

Imagine Columbus's pitch: *I'm going to sail in a direction from which nobody has ever returned, toward a destination not on the map. I don't know how long it will take or what we will discover. Give me money and ships and men who will die if I am wrong.*

It worked! Columbus got his ships and his crew, and ultimately a day when all the banks close. He had nobody to copy, but his actions changed the world.[47] *Columbus was an entrepreneur!* All the problems I had were just little versions of what he had. My employees needed health insurance; his employees needed vitamin C. My employees wanted me out of their meetings; his employees wanted to kill him.

And then, so suddenly that I almost spilled my red wine, I realized how I could find my mentor. I just had to *look*

---

[47] And not all would say for the better.

back in time. Entrepreneurs are rare. The ones who are alive are so fantastically busy that they have no time to chat. But once I got over my prejudice against being dead,[48] the search for a mentor became far easier.

Some Time Travel

I had spent my whole career looking for mentors not in the wrong place but at the wrong time. Successful entrepreneurs and their Innovation Stacks leave huge marks on the world; therefore, history must be full of them. And so it was. I had been trying to find other entrepreneurs by looking at other businesses. But this was like trying to see the stars from a city. There is so much dust and light pollution that only a few stars appear.[49] But go away from the dust and the light of the city and the sky reveals a million sharp points of light.

Think about the events humankind chooses to record. The most significant are chronicled and everything else is forgotten. History is basically selection bias in written form. Innovation Stacks are rare, but when they do occur they create organizations with massive impact and longevity. No surprise, then, that the history books are full of examples. Looking back in time I saw so many examples of entrepreneurship it was overwhelming. But at least now I had some data!

---

[48] Columbus himself looked to the past for inspiration just like I was looking: everywhere he went, he took his heavily annotated 1485 edition of Marco Polo's *Book of Marvels.*

[49] Nope, it's moving; that's a 737.

I had originally thought that what happened to us at Square was such an anomaly that it was almost irrelevant, but looking back in time I found so many similar examples it was almost commonplace. With literally thousands of examples to choose from, I could be picky in choosing my mentors. I had the luxury of so much data that I could run a proper study. Dad would be proud.

My main criterion was that the industry not be at all related to technology. Moore's Law, viral growth, and other tech-related phenomena are so powerful that they could skew the data. There are, in fact, many great tech companies employing Innovation Stacks, but are the results from the tech or the Stack? It made more sense to study the Innovation Stack's effect on "boring" industries where any impacts would be stark.

I decided to choose three stars at which to point the telescope, and the first would be the hardest to discover. I wanted to find another Square. I wanted a US financial company founded by outsiders for the purpose of including people who had been shut out. This firm should have had nearly the same journey, just without any computers. I found the perfect example only a ten-minute walk from Square's headquarters in San Francisco, give or take a century.

For my next example, I wanted one of the most common industries in the world. This industry should have been around for thousands of years, so that all the innovation had a few millennia to surface. I also wanted an industry that touched nearly everyone across the globe and was as low tech as possible.

For my final case study, I wanted the worst industry imaginable. This would be a ruthlessly competitive industry that had destroyed more fortunes than it created. Like a game of chess or go, no company could have a technological edge over any opponent because everyone had exactly the same pieces. Finally, the industry should be highly regulated to demonstrate the power of an Innovation Stack even when creativity was suppressed.

One of the challenges of seeing Innovation Stacks in history is that over time they become industries of their own. While the originator of the Stack may enjoy a massive advantage for decades, eventually other firms will copy it. In fact, this is why my first mentor was so hard to find: his Innovation Stack was so successful that it eventually *became* the whole industry.

And so we must now travel a century back in time and meet my first mentor, A. P. Giannini. A man who cast such a large shadow over the financial world that Square had been standing in it the entire time.

CHAPTER 9

The Bank of Italy

To illustrate the power and timelessness of the Innovation Stack, I want to tell you the story of a bank. Not just any bank, but one that created an Innovation Stack so powerful that it became the largest bank in the world. In doing so, it opened the world of finance to hundreds of millions of people and built much of the western United States. In fact, the things we now associate with a bank—branches, savings, checking, small loans, etc.—were originally part of a century-old Innovation Stack. But bank stories, let's face it, are boring.

Instead, I'm going to tell you the story of a superhero. It's a story of travel and adventure. There is an evil gang, murder, espionage, and of course the destruction of a major city. Death and mayhem, you got it! The hero is a handsome, hazel-eyed giant with a booming voice who occasionally even wore a cape, something men in the 1800s could do without irony or stretchy pants. The story is so epic that my original draft of this chapter was a graphic novel.[50] Unfortunately, e-readers and audiobooks cannot adequately reproduce the drama of ink on newsprint, so I've reverted to the written word. Format notwithstanding, get ready to meet the most awesome banker in history.

A. P. Giannini

In 1869, twenty-two-year-old Luigi Giannini and his fourteen-year-old wife, Virginia, arrived in San Jose, California, having crossed the country on the new transcontinental railroad. Their baby, Amadeo Pietro (A.P.), was born in 1870. The hardworking young couple ran a hotel and soon saved enough to purchase a forty-acre farm in the fertile Santa Clara Valley.

Luigi was a good farmer, and Virginia was a good manager. The farm prospered and the family grew, with a baby brother and another on the way. But then, returning from the fields one afternoon, A.P. and his father were confronted by an angry farmhand. With his six-year-old son watching, Luigi was shot dead over a $1 dispute. Our young superhero learned in the worst possible way how tragic money problems could be.

His now twenty-one-year-old mother ran the farm and raised her three sons, but soon married Lorenzo Scatena, a produce trader. Produce trading was a thrilling business in

---

[50] A copy of the graphic novel is at jimmckelvey.com. If you wish, you can download it, get some popcorn, and just skip the rest of this chapter.

the days before refrigeration, and young A.P. was hooked. At fifteen he joined his stepfather's firm.

A.P.'s work ethic was legendary. Waking before dawn, he would travel out to farms others considered too remote, helping those farmers get their crops to market. One day A.P. saw a competitor ahead of him heading to a farm across a river. There was no time to travel to the bridge before his competitor got there, so A.P. tied his horse and swam the river, holding his clothes above his head. By the time his dry competition arrived, A.P. and the farmer had already signed a contract.

Does swimming a river sound insane? I have twice sneaked onto a sold-out flight to make it to an important meeting.[51] I also once stripped my way into a contract with the Institute of Transportation Engineers.[52] I'm not justifying either action, just making the point that a naked man swimming a river to buy some almonds makes perfect sense to me.

A.P. was the older brother I always wanted.

Scatena & Sons soon became the largest produce company in the West. By age thirty-one A.P. had more than enough money to live on for the rest of his life, so he retired and joined the board of a bank.

But banking in 1901 was not like banking today. The banks ignored small businesses, forcing desperate people into the hands of loan sharks or out of business entirely.

---

[51] This was before September 11 and increased airport security.
[52] I'll put the details, but no photos, at jimmckelvey.com.

A.P. tried to persuade his fellow directors to change their ways, but failed. In frustration, he quit the board and ran across town to another bank where a friend of his worked. "I'm going to open a bank for people who don't use banks. Giacomo, tell me how to do it." A.P. named it the Bank of Italy.

WHEN I FIRST HEARD the stories of A. P. Giannini,[53] I knew I had found the right star. We even chose the same city. One hundred five years before this glassblower and a massage therapist[54] launched a credit card processor, here was a produce trader launching a bank. Our motivations were nearly identical: we wanted to include more people and square up an unfair system. Another similarity was that we had no idea what we were doing.

Our respective decisions to square up the system for people who had been excluded was the moment our paths diverged from all the other credit card processors and banks. By choosing to build a system that could serve "the little fellow,"[55] as A.P. would say, we were also choosing to build an Innovation Stack. Metaphorically, all three of us had left the walled city; but A.P. was about to literally run back into a burning one.

---

[53] Gerald Nash. *A. P. Giannini and the Bank of America* (Norman: University of Oklahoma Press, 1992).
[54] Jack Dorsey is a professionally credentialed massage therapist.
[55] *Wild West*, October 2016, p. 22.

The Great Quake

At 5:12 a.m. on April 18, 1906, the hand of fate threw A.P. and everyone in his family out of bed. The Great San Francisco Earthquake was strong enough to be felt in Canada, but A.P.'s house in San Mateo remained standing. With his family safe, he dressed quickly and headed into San Francisco to check on his fledgling Bank of Italy.

Initially, the city appeared to have survived. Some buildings fell from the shaking, but the vast majority of structures were made of wood, and wooden structures withstand shaking better than brick. Of course, wood does have some drawbacks.

In my living room sits a pile of dry wood suspended above a porous gas pipe and a source of flame. We call this collection of objects a "self-starting fireplace," but in 1906 it was called "the City of San Francisco." The brittle gas lines running underground were broken by the quake, sending plumes of explosive gas to the lamps lighting the wooden buildings. Thirty separate, simultaneous fires erupted throughout the city. As a cruel joke, the same forces that broke the gas lines also ruptured the water lines, removing any hope that the residents could fight the flames. San Francisco would burn, it was just a matter of when.

A.P. arrived at noon, five hours after leaving his home, to find the Bank of Italy open and unharmed. A.P. had seen the fires on his trip into town and knew they were coming deeper into the city. But it was not just the gas and water lines that were severed; the thin threads that support civilization had snapped as well. With the police and firefighters overwhelmed by a burning city, lawlessness spread faster than the flames. Gangs of looters rampaged and the tiny Bank of Italy had no fire safe, just a lockbox and one revolver.

A.P. sent a clerk to Scatena & Sons to get two horse-drawn produce carts, complete with old produce. They loaded the bank's gold and records onto the carts and then hid the treasure under the vegetables to disguise it from the looters. They waited until sunset, then under the cover of darkness they drove the horses seventeen miles to A.P.'s home. He hid the gold in the ash trap of the family fireplace.

Finally, here's a person an entrepreneur can relate to. I've never faced looters and a burning city, but I did once smuggle forty thousand banned CD-ROMs across a picket line and security gate in a monster truck. The truck was so jacked up off the ground and looked so ridiculous they never bothered to look inside the tailgate. But my mentor's tale stands alone. Right down to A.P. remarking that afterward, "our money smelled like orange juice for weeks."

Two days after the earthquake, with smoke still lingering over the city, the leaders of all the banks in San Francisco met and chose a course of action: actually, *inaction*—they decided to stay closed for six months. A.P. was furious! Now was the time people needed money and loans to rebuild the city. While the other banks froze in fear, A.P. and the Bank of Italy went down to the wharf with a bag of gold and a ledger book. He began lending money to anyone who wanted to rebuild San Francisco.

THE INNOVATION STACK that the Bank of Italy built has an uncanny resemblance to what we created at Square a century later. We created innovation to make the system easier to use and accessible to everyone. There were new systems built to encourage rapid growth and word-of-mouth advertising. There were new risk and underwriting systems. We even had to fight and plead with regulators to change some of the rules. See if any of this looks familiar.

The Bank of Italy's Innovation Stack

1. **Focus on "the Little Fellow."** A.P. said, "It is our purpose to make a specialty of the interest of the small depositor and borrower. We consider the wage earner or small business man who deposits his savings regularly, no matter how small the amount may be, to be the most valuable client our bank can have."[56] But many "small business men" were not men, *so they had to* have . . .

2. **Banking for Women.** After the 19th Amendment gave women the right to vote, Bank of Italy opened the country's first bank for women, the Women's Banking Department. It was located in an upper floor at Giannini's

---

[56] Marquis James and Bessie R. James. *The Story of Bank of America: Biography of a Bank* (Washington, DC: Beard Books, 2002), p. 64.

new bank building on Powell Street in San Francisco. For the first time in America, women had access to their own accounts and could manage their finances without involvement of their spouses. But many of these new men and women customers were very thrifty, *so they had to have . . .*

3. **Low Rates.** As Square would later do, Bank of Italy set its fees far below those of its peers. While competitors charged 12 percent interest, Bank of Italy charged 7 percent. This caused both massive growth in loan volume and the need to attract depositors. It also attracted a more frugal and responsible clientele. A.P. said, "You are putting borrowers out of business if you charge 10 or 12 percent. The man who will fight for cheaper interest rates is the one we want to loan money to."[57] But low rates meant they needed high volumes, *so they had to build a . . .*

4. **Direct Sales Force.** Bank of Italy sent salesmen door-to-door and to every wedding, church picnic, baptism, and social event in the neighborhood. Banks at the time didn't actively sell their services, but perhaps they should have because it worked beautifully. The effect of the direct sales force was most noticeable in later years when the Bank of Italy took over another bank. The number of accounts would double within a year.

---

[57] *The Story of Bank of America*, p. 83.

But salespeople are more effective if people have heard of what they are selling, *so they had to* begin . . .

5. **Advertising.** No other banks advertised at the time, but in its very first year Bank of Italy began to reach out. One advertisement read:

ONE DOLLAR—It is not much—but it is worth saving. With one dollar you can open a savings account which may be the beginning of your fortune. If in this moment you have one dollar which you may either spend thoughtlessly or place in a safe place, come to our bank and deposit it. It will earn interest together with other funds which you may be able to deposit.

Advertising to small savers would mean nothing if they could not open an account with the small amount of money they had, *so they had to* set . . .

6. **Low Minimums.** Most other banks required much more than $1 to open an account. Bank of Italy made it easy for everyone to open an account. As the small depositors grew, so did the bank's resources. But with so many new small customers, the bank had to streamline the sign-up process, *so they had to* create . . .

7. **Simplified Underwriting.** The paperwork required for a Bank of Italy account was far simpler than for other banks. Especially after the earthquake and fire,

sometimes a handshake was sufficient. Giannini would sometimes lend to people he knew without paperwork or credit checks. His branch managers had authority to make loans based on more than just raw numbers; they could also consider a person's character. But having a friendly staff is not helpful if nobody understands them, *so they had to* hire . . .

8. **Multilingual Tellers.** Many of these new customers were immigrants who spoke little English. Bank of Italy had tellers who spoke the native languages of their customers. But it's hard—and intimidating—to speak with someone behind iron bars and glass, *so they had to* have . . .

9. **Open Floorplans.** The insides of the Bank of Italy branches were open and friendly. Tellers and managers were seated up front, not behind iron bars or sequestered on special floors. A.P. always put his own desk at the very front of the bank. It was a friendly place people wanted to visit, and visit often, *so they had to* have . . .

10. **Expanded Hours.** Bank of Italy kept hours that matched people's lives. Many working people were at their jobs when normal banks were open, so Giannini kept the schedule of his customers. When Bank of Italy opened its first branch on August 1, 1907, it had evening and even Sunday hours. With so many families banking with them, they needed to consider the most significant asset most families own, *so they had to* offer . . .

11. **Home Mortgages.** Bank of Italy made loans on people's homes before this practice was common. This helped not only the new home owners but everyone else in the real estate business, from the builders to the furniture makers, whom Bank of Italy also served. Home lending was so successful that they soon expanded to . . .

12. **Auto Loans.** As people became more prosperous, they wanted their own transportation. Bank of Italy made the first car loans and also financed the car dealers, driving a wheel of demand. The car is an asset that can be used as collateral, but it depreciates so fast that the loan mostly depends on the character of the borrower. Once Bank of Italy figured out how to make loans based on the borrower and not the asset, *they had to* offer . . .

13. **Installment Credit.** Radical for a bank, but life-changing for an individual, installment credit kept people out of the grip of loan sharks when trouble hit. This created massive goodwill, further fueling Bank of Italy's growth, *so they had to* have . . .

14. **Rapid Expansion.** The combined effects of all this innovation drove the need for rapid expansion. Bank of Italy would sometimes build new banks, but preferred to buy existing banks. This gave them both local knowledge and a ready workforce. But with the addition of so many new banks, *they had to* evolve perhaps their most powerful element . . .

15. Branch Banking. Banking tied to a specific region was risky—a disaster could strike a whole area, creating a wave of loan defaults. On the other hand, having multiple locations provided tremendous efficiencies. Stable areas had excess savings, and growing areas had excess demand. One agricultural region may have had drought while elsewhere there were bumper crops. A branch banking system balanced these forces in a way no single bank could and gave the financial power of a massive corporation to even the smallest towns.

Branch banking made so much financial sense that Bank of Italy went on a buying spree. They would find a town, buy a bank, then apply their Innovation Stack. To finance all this expansion, *they had to* create . . .

16. Distributed Ownership. This massive growth required massive capital. Bank of Italy pioneered a way of selling tiny amounts of stock to large numbers of people, giving both inspiration and wealth to employees and customers. A.P. insisted that no individual or institution own more than a few percentage points, including himself. This made fundraising more cumbersome, but it protected the bank from a single powerful entity during times of trouble. A.P. not only built an institution to serve "the little fellow," he also let that little fellow own it.

A century before it was cool for employees to own a piece of the business, Bank of Italy was selling stock to its people.

Not only did it help these people, but it more than once saved the bank from hostile forces that tried to seize control.

My First Mentor

If the preceding sixteen interrelated elements seem boring or obvious, that's because you didn't grow up a century ago. At the time this was radical innovation. Having a safe place to save and access to loans as necessary changes lives and builds nations. Giannini was despised by other bankers, who considered him reckless and radical for enabling everyone to bank. They may even have told him so over a multi-martini meal.

The fact that almost every bank today has copied the Bank of Italy, which later became the Bank of America, is a testament to the power of entrepreneurship and inclusion. An entrepreneur's audacity and perseverance can eventually dominate an industry so totally that the battle grows quiet again.

But don't be fooled. Many things we now consider commonplace had a dramatic beginning. A. P. Giannini's original Innovation Stack is now the model for most modern banks. In an effort to provide a bank "for the little fellow," Giannini built the largest bank in the world. It turns out there are a lot more "little fellows" than big shots. Building an Innovation Stack that can successfully serve the smallest, poorest customers gives you exclusive access to a massive market.

Giannini's experience was remarkably similar to ours at Square, beginning with his decision to enter an industry that he knew nothing about. We both entered industries that had been designed to serve a select group. We saw injustice and cowardice and abuse. We had no idea how to fix it. But even to us outsiders, some basic problems were obvious. Our systems had to welcome, even encourage, people who had previously been excluded. So we rebelled and rebuilt.

Once I saw this pattern that we'd lived through at Square repeated in the life of a man I had never met, it all made sense. It made sense that I could never find a mentor among the living, because at any point in time, there are only a few people who are both innovative *and* successful. (And good luck getting a coffee date with one of them.) It made sense that this kind of mentor would be as rare as world-changing businesses are. It made sense that most of them wouldn't be alive during my lifetime. While most people become successful by emulating other successful people, I had taken a different path.

But reverse the lens of time and the names of successful entrepreneurs dominate the history books. If one thousand crazy people tried something a hundred years ago, the three who succeeded became household names. And we love to write about those people because they opened opportunities for us all. Plus, they succeeded against the odds, which makes a great story.

Pick just about any industry and you can see the pattern. An entrepreneur begins a journey in an area where there is no market. He or she is forced to solve a series of problems, which results in an Innovation Stack. The Innovation Stack, combined with the first-mover advantage, combined with some other tricks we will discuss in the coming chapters, creates a world-changing enterprise.

But looking backward in time revealed so many examples of Innovation Stacks that I became overwhelmed. Now, instead of too little data, I had too much. My problem became choosing from among so many good examples, which allowed me to choose an exciting example from a boring industry.

If you want to study a subject, a plain background helps. Without all the drama and explosions, the true effects are easier to see. So, for our next example, let's examine the most boring industry in history.

CHAPTER 10

The Boy They Kicked Out

WHAT happened at Square now seemed less like an accident. Learning the story of A. P. Giannini and the Bank of Italy made me feel like I finally found a wise older brother. The parallels between Square and the Bank of Italy seemed too obvious to ignore, but there was still one serious problem with my research.

As mentioned, my original draft of the last chapter was a graphic novel, and Giannini fit the profile of a superhero nicely. *That* was the problem. Giannini was such a powerful figure that I could not discount the possibility that it was his sheer drive and ingenuity, and not the power of the Innovation Stack, that produced such epic results. This is a common problem outside the laboratory—there are too many variables that can affect the outcome.

To really prove the power of an Innovation Stack required me to find another test case. This time I needed to find both a special industry and a special entrepreneur. With all of human history to choose from, there are hundreds of examples of the Innovation Stack at work, so I purposely sought one with the *least* drama. No murders, no burning city, no caped heroes. But more important: no computers, no viral growth, and no network effect.

The tech industry is exciting and great at creating fortunes, but it does terrible things to data. Study a successful tech company in any particular industry and it is hard to separate out the effects of the technology. This is why I laugh when people copy Google's management practices. Twenty billion dollars of free cash flow fixes a lot of managerial mistakes. Google may have the best management in the world, but how do you control for the fact that the company can also fund its own space program?

I wanted exciting data, so I chose a mundane industry, one that has been around since hominids discovered cutting tools. Surely in a business predating the written word all the innovation must have already happened. I picked a business that has thousands of competitors in every part of the world so the playing field would be perfectly level. A business that is so "boring" that it actually becomes a fascinating example of innovation.

But the entrepreneur was just as important as the industry for this new test case. I didn't want another caped hero, but the opposite. I wanted someone who was introverted and shy. Someone who might have happily stayed within the walled city, had he not been driven out. I found a Swedish boy who fit the bill perfectly. Actually, too well. Far from a hero, I found a villain.

A year before starting a world-changing company at age seventeen, this boy joined a Swedish pro-Nazi party. He later emphatically renounced this decision, but his association with the horrors of fascism made me look for a less repugnant example. I ultimately chose to include this story not as an example of entrepreneurial heroics, but to demonstrate the powerful good that an Innovation Stack can have even in the hands of someone who might not be motivated to help the disenfranchised. The story was included because we can see the power of the Innovation Stack without attributing its impact to the charisma or benevolence of the entrepreneur.

IKEA

One day in 1943, a seventeen-year-old Swedish boy named Ingvar Kamprad bicycled from his family farm, called Elmtaryd, into town. Kamprad filled out a form and sent it to the Agunnaryd city council with a ten-krona note. Thus was Ikéa (Ingvar Kamprad, Elmtaryd, Agunnaryd) formed—the firm would change the spelling to IKEA later.

Kamprad began by selling matchboxes: his aunt helped him buy them in a lot of one hundred boxes for eighty-eight öre, and the enterprising young Kamprad sold the boxes for two or three öre each. After forming IKEA as a teenager, Kamprad went on the road with the firm's first major offering, fountain pens, traveling by train to small shops throughout southern Sweden. For the first few years, the firm sold pens, Christmas cards, picture frames, stockings, seeds, and other knickknacks.[58]

---

[58] Ingvar Kamprad and Bertil Torekull. *Leading by Design: The IKEA Story* (New York: Harper Business, 2011), p. 47.

Over the next five years, Kamprad did what most businesspeople do: he copied his competition. The first result of all this copying was that IKEA became a mail-order business: customers would send in a form, and the factories that produced the items would deliver them to the customer. IKEA's biggest mail-order competitor, Gunnars Fabriker, then began selling furniture, so IKEA copied that idea as well. Both catalogs, in fact, sold many of the same items and the result was an inevitable price war.

Racing to the Bottom

For instance, the Melby ironing board was sold in both the Gunnars and the IKEA catalogs. IKEA began selling this ironing board for twenty-three kronor, before being undersold by Gunnars, where it was offered for a half krona less. IKEA then dropped its price to twenty-two kronor, and the race to the bottom continued. Kamprad described how.[59]

> Step by step, this price war affected the quality of the ironing boards, which became simpler and simpler, but also worse and worse. The same applied to furniture. Complaints started to mount, and I could see how things were going: the mail-order trade was risking an increasingly bad reputation and in the long run IKEA could not survive in that way. The core problem with mail order was that the customers

---

[59] *Leading by Design*, p. 52.

themselves could not touch the goods but had to rely on descriptions in the advertisement or catalog. Consumer protection was poorly developed, and it was easy to cheat. We were faced with a momentous decision: to allow IKEA to die or to find a new way of maintaining the trust of the customer and still make money.

It was an existential threat. The two catalogs would always undercut each other on the same products, driving both quality and profits out of the system. Kamprad didn't see a solution. But Kamprad's competitors were about to help him solve this problem: not by giving him something else to copy, but by preventing him from copying altogether. Kamprad was about to become an entrepreneur.

Kicked Out and Kept Out

Beginning in 1950, bowing to pressure from other Swedish furniture sellers, IKEA was banned from furniture trade fairs. A furniture fair might not sound like the hottest ticket in town, but these were important events for both sellers and buyers. They showcased what was new and provided an opportunity for dealers and suppliers to interact. And at a certain point, they were opened up to the public as well. And not only was IKEA kept from exhibiting; Kamprad *himself* was personally forbidden from attending. He did his best to circumvent this, once by being smuggled past the gates of a show in Göteborg under a carpet.

In Stockholm, he rented space near the St. Erik's Fair to show IKEA's furniture to the public. His display was mobbed. Everyone was curious about the firm with the forbidden furniture. No doubt some customers read banned books while waiting in line.

Following the success of his rented space, Kamprad decided to gamble on a permanent location and solve two problems at once. He needed to both show his goods and demonstrate their quality. Kamprad wanted people to see the furniture for themselves, actually touch the pieces and compare them, to better understand what they'd be getting for their money. So he bought an old building, cleared it out, installed new windows, and built a permanent display of his company's furniture.

IKEA's first catalog exclusively dedicated to furniture invited customers to come to this old building and see for themselves. And they came—a line of a thousand people stretched outside the showroom the first day it opened in 1953. Kamprad and his small staff worried that the floors might collapse like a cheap ironing board. But the floors held, and people kept coming, tens of thousands that first year, from all around the country. Finally, the ironing board problem was solved. As Kamprad later recalled, "We could now at last show those cheap ironing boards alongside those that cost five kronor more and were of good quality. And people did just what we had hoped: they wisely chose the more expensive ironing board."[60]

---

[60] *Leading by Design*, p. 53.

But Kamprad's competitors were not done with their attacks. Not only were IKEA and its owner banned from trade fairs, the other Swedish furniture sellers soon organized a boycott of IKEA's suppliers. "We were driven to Poland because in free-enterprise Sweden there was a furniture trade that started a boycott against us because of our low prices,"[61] Kamprad recalled.

The effect of all these attacks was to turn a modest Swede into the world's most successful furniture entrepreneur. "I had many tearful nights when I sensed that the very existence of the firm was threatened. That also gave birth to a greater determination to fight and find ways out," Kamprad said. "New problems created a dizzying chance. When we were not allowed to buy the same furniture that others were, we were forced to design our own, and that came to provide us with a style of our own, a design of our own. And from the necessity to secure our own deliveries, a chance arose that in its turn opened up a whole new world to us."[62]

And so, driven by bans and boycotts, IKEA created an Innovation Stack that changed the furniture industry.

IKEA's Innovation Stack

1. **Catalog Showrooms.** As with other entrepreneurial
   firms, IKEA was forced to evolve an Innovation Stack

---

[61] *Leading by Design*, p. 214.
[62] *Leading by Design*, p. 84.

in response to a harsh environment. Kamprad explained a key element of IKEA's Innovation Stack:

At that moment, the basis of the modern IKEA concept was created, and in principle still applies: first and foremost, use a catalog to tempt people to come to an exhibition, which today is our store. Second, we provided a large building within which, catalog in hand, customers could walk around and see simple interiors for themselves, touch the furniture they wanted to buy, and then write out an order which would be put into effect by mail via the factories. Mail order and furniture store in one. As far as I knew, that business idea had not been put into practice anywhere else. We were the first.[63]

But they couldn't make this furniture in their home country, *so they had to* begin . . .

2. **Overseas Manufacturing.** With the factories of Sweden closed to IKEA from the boycott, Kamprad had to go elsewhere, so he chose a place with low labor costs and good natural resources, Poland. The economy of Poland was a mess, so IKEA was able to hire great workers for a fraction of the cost of Swedish workers. But the Polish factories were antiquated and had quality problems, *so they had to* build . . .

---

[63] *Leading by Design.*

3. **Efficient Factories.** Redesigning the Polish factories not only solved the quality problem, but also increased efficiency and lowered costs. The factories made so much furniture that shipping volumes grew massively. But shipping bulky furniture from Poland was inefficient and expensive because the furniture packages were mostly empty space, *so they had to* create . . .

4. **Knocked-Down Furniture.** Knocked-down furniture saved shipping space and reduced damage. But it required workers on the receiving end to reassemble it, and these workers added labor costs and just created another delivery problem for the final customer, *so they had to* create . . .

5. **Self-Assembled Furniture.** IKEA had the idea to keep prices low and save time and space by asking customers to assemble the furniture themselves. But knocked-down furniture was difficult for customers to assemble, *so they had to* add . . .

6. **Custom Design.** To solve the problem of furniture that was difficult to assemble, IKEA built its own staff of furniture designers. But these designers did more than simplify the final assembly process; they also worked directly with IKEA's factories to design furniture that was efficient to produce in their customized Polish factories, lowering costs even more. And the

designers were able to optimize raw materials across IKEA's entire product line, *so now they had* . . .

7. **Interchangeable Parts.** One screw could be used on thousands of final products. This helped customers assemble furniture by making the basic steps similar even for very different products. Standardizing on a limited set of parts also allowed IKEA to simplify its inventory and achieve economies of scale. But IKEA's volume soon exceeded what the original Polish factories could produce, *so they had to* build a . . .

8. **Global Supply Chain.** IKEA's growth and volume allowed it to choose whatever spot on the planet was best to produce a certain item. This efficiency saved money and simplified the tasks that any one factory had to perform. It also created an inventory problem, as all these goods had to be stored somewhere, *so they had to* invent . . .

9. **Warehouse Showrooms.** Knocked-down, self-assembled furniture was so space efficient that IKEA could store it in warehouses attached to the showrooms. This saved shipping costs, plus it allowed customers to get their products immediately, instead of waiting months for the factory to deliver a custom order. But with all this success, the stores were getting so big that people were getting lost in them, *so they had to* build . . .

10. **Winding Paths.** IKEA's departments are cleverly spaced along a winding path. This helps the store seem less intimidating and allows customers to see the range of products. People will travel hours or even days just to shop at IKEA. But now people were spending more time in the stores, *so they had to* provide . . .

11. **Food and Child Care.** You can spend a day shopping at IKEA, and now there is no reason to leave the store. Eat a meal, drop the kids into the ball pit, then prepare to look at thousands of different products all with IKEA's . . .

12. **Low Prices.** IKEA shares all the efficiency of this stacked innovation with its customers through its low prices. People know and trust the IKEA brand and the value it represents.

Squaring Up Furniture

Kamprad explained how it fit together with one Allen key.

> I had a kind of awakening on the idea level when I went to the Milan Fair and visited a large carpet supplier. Thanks to him, I was able to see ordinary Italian households, the homes of simple clerks and workers. What I saw surprised me: heavy, dark furniture, a single light bulb above a heavy dining room table; a

chasm between all the elegance at the fair and what could be seen in the homes of ordinary people.

It is hard to say when a philosophy begins to take shape in a person's head. I don't want to exaggerate my farsightedness, but I think Milan gave me a shove in the direction toward . . . "democratic design": that is, a design that was not just good but also from the start adapted to machine production and thus cheap to produce. With a design of that kind, and the innovation of self-assembly, we could save a great deal of money in the factories and on transport, as well as keep down the price to the customer.[64]

Kamprad eventually distilled his vision of squaring up the furniture market into IKEA's Business Motto: *We shall offer a wide range of home furnishing items of good design and function at prices so low that the majority of people can afford to buy them.*[65]

And there it was, the Innovation Stack and the desire to square up (politics notwithstanding). But I was interested more in IKEA's process than its profits. Neither Square nor IKEA chose the path of innovation immediately. Square went to copy the best practices of the credit card industry that we found, but we abandoned that idea halfway through our first day after realizing that the existing system could

---

[64] *Leading by Design*, p. 88.
[65] *Leading by Design*, p. 172.

never serve the people we wanted to serve. Similarly, IKEA tried to be like other furniture stores in many ways, but was blocked from the trade fairs and factories and ultimately its homeland.

The seventeen-year-old boy who was kicked out of the city built the biggest furniture store in history. IKEA's Innovation Stack is the perfect illustration of how innovation can transform even the most undramatic industry in the world. IKEA is a staggeringly successful business and is certainly wildly profitable, but just how profitable is unknown since IKEA is a private company.[66]

Kamprad also fascinated me. Here was this now reformed and mild-mannered man who in many ways seemed like the opposite of Giannini. I tried to contact Ingvar Kamprad to learn his story firsthand. Unfortunately, he died as I was still researching this book.

It is one thing to piece a historical set of facts into a theory; it is quite another to present that theory to a person who has lived the experience. So, for my final industry to study, I wanted not only to find great data, but also to learn from a person who was there.

I not only found another perfect company to study, but its founder was still alive. And I mean *really* alive.

---

[66] Actually, it is dozens of companies spread across the globe.

CHAPTER 11

The Cloud God

JIM! It's Herb Kelleher."[67]
I had spent months trying to contact the famous former CEO of Southwest Airlines. Herb doesn't do email. To reach him, I contacted his office in Dallas, described this book project, left my phone number, and then waited. Herb doesn't do calendar invites. His voice is so powerful that I was certain it had just voided my phone's warranty. "So you want to hear the Southwest story. Come on down to Dallas and I'll tell you all about it." Herb doesn't do teleconferences.

I've met movie stars, Nobel laureates, and heads of state, but I was more excited to meet Herb than any of them. Southwest Airlines, the company he had led for thirty years, was the perfect test case of my theories. In an industry seemingly designed to keep every company lumped together in an undifferentiated scrum, here was one that literally flew in

---

[67] All quotations from Herb Kelleher are from a visit in his Dallas office on February 2, 2017.

the face of convention. If a scientist could choose a market for a case study of entrepreneurship and Innovation Stacks, it would be commercial aviation, precisely because the industry is so terrible.

But did it fit? I had spent three years after the Amazon battle collecting data, but was never able to show it to someone who had actually been there. A great thing about data, especially historical data, is there is nobody alive to contradict you. Would Abraham Lincoln *really* have chosen that bank? Would Albert Einstein *really* have used that hair gel? We really can't know. Studying history is fantastic until you want to ask a question of one of the characters. I worried that my theories would not survive the scrutiny of someone who had actually been there.

Herb was legendary, and flying Southwest down to the airline's Dallas headquarters made the legend loom larger. The airport itself is on Herb Kelleher Way. I walked into Southwest's lobby and saw a giant monitor with the airline's current on-time performance, then I noticed something odd. The Central Time Zone had been renamed "Herb Time." Even after a decade of retirement, Herb got his own time zone, and a special executive suite at headquarters.

To understand what an amazing creation Southwest Airlines was, you first have to understand how horrible the airline industry was when Southwest entered the fray. It was, quite simply, the worst industry in the world. Herb actually had a study from a Wharton professor who, after researching various industries for thirty-two years, ranked airlines dead last.[68] But even someone without tenure can see that the financial history of aviation is uglier than a mid-air collision.

The Wright brothers themselves could not make money in the sky despite having a worldwide monopoly on airplanes. A look at balance sheets from 1903 to yesterday might make you think people weren't *meant* to go hurtling through the air. Whatever unseen force keeps planes aloft, it certainly isn't the invisible hand of capitalism.

The entire industry lost money consistently until one day in 1967 when a tiny airline started up in Texas. Southwest Airlines then set decades' worth of records, not just in aviation, but in business too. It entered the worst industry imaginable, was attacked mercilessly for years, and loved it. Under Herb's leadership Southwest had the lowest fares, happiest customers, best on-time record, fastest growth, and highest profits. And Herb can prove it.

Herb's office suite is a trophy case of memorabilia, but with a twist. For every formal award there are a dozen homemade gifts from Southwest employees and customers, mostly heart shaped in honor of the corporate logo. Here was a company so loved by its people that they took the time to make the boss a heartfelt felt heart. To stand among these hundreds of gifts was both friendly and intimidating, sort of like Herb. Herb is charming and funny, but he also has

---

[68] Herb pointed out to this professor several additional ways in which airlines were even worse than he had calculated.

the aura of a deity: an image only enhanced by his deep baritone that seems to emanate from a cloud. He custom builds these clouds from a continuous stream of Kool Blue Menthol cigarette smoke. A high cirrus layer hovered over his office as we began talking.

The Federal Airline Protection System

My first goal was to learn why Southwest didn't just copy the other airlines. "The airlines set up federal government regulation in 1938 to protect themselves from competition," Herb explained to me, "and they were enormously successful because the airlines that had 90 percent of all the revenue passenger miles in 1938 had 90 percent of all the revenue passenger miles in 1978."

So the US government not only forbade innovation, but also forbade entering the market in the first place. The only legal path to the skies went through the courts. Herb did not actually start out as an airline executive or a businessperson; he was Southwest's lawyer. Herb fought the government and the airlines for four years before Southwest could make its first flight. The battle took them to both the Texas and the US Supreme Courts. When Southwest Airlines finally won, Herb cried and kissed the first airplane.

Copying was almost forced on the industry by government regulation. Any carrier would have to fly within the government's rules. And these rules had a strange side effect: they not only discouraged innovation, they actually changed the way people thought.

"There was a growing consensus in Washington that only rich people and people on corporate expense account *wanted* to fly." My jaw almost landed in his ashtray, but Herb kept going: "I am serious. I used that word deliberately, because I saw the look on your face.

"When I first got into litigation involving the Civil Aeronautics Board lawyers, I thought they were just kidding when they were saying things like, 'None of these people want to fly.' Well, let me see, if we can take you from that Rio Grande Valley to the MD Anderson Cancer Center in Houston on an airplane in forty-five minutes for $15, I think I would choose that over being put on the mattress in the back of the station wagon and being driven for six hours. I thought that they were just making it up, but they weren't."

Living behind a wall long enough not only causes people to become comfortable with their circumstances, but they also start to believe there is nothing beyond the wall. Why would Bob, for example, want to accept a credit card, or have a bank account, or own nice furniture, or visit his grandma? *Why would normal people want something that only the wealthy have?*

Southwest eventually won the right to fly, but that victory only allowed them to fly certain routes within Texas. They were still legally prevented from copying much of what the other carriers were doing. Southwest was born outside the wall.

Herb confirmed it. "We were not going to copy. We may do the same things operationally; after all we are all flying airplanes. But fundamentally we decided we won't do anything the way the legacy carriers did." Howard Putnam, a former vice president at United Airlines and Southwest's CEO for three years, once said that the greatest thing he ever did for Southwest was "not implementing anything I learned at United."[69]

So there it was, audacity. Southwest would provide low-cost air travel and would not copy the other carriers. Herb had confirmed what I'd identified as the most basic component of entrepreneurship: solving a perfect problem. In this case, they were going to open up the world of air travel to everyone. I felt like I was floating on a beautiful menthol cloud.

Not only did Herb confirm my theory, he went on to explain how all the attacks and battles made the company stronger. Southwest had to deal with federal regulation and over thirty administrative and judicial hearings, while also withstanding a barrage of other attacks that were actively:

- Excluding Southwest from the airline credit card system.
- Blocking access to refueling hydrants.
- Boycotting vendors who worked with Southwest.
- Limiting Southwest's routes through federal legislation.[70]

---

[69] Kevin Freiberg and Jackie Freiberg. *Nuts!: Southwest Airlines' Crazy Recipe for Business and Personal Success* (New York: Crown, 1998).
[70] The Wright Amendment forbade Southwest from flying from Dallas Love Field to any noncontiguous state.

The attacks were so extreme that Braniff and Texas International were indicted in 1975 for conspiring to put Southwest out of business. They pled no contest and paid $100,000 in fines. Ultimately, all these attacks just strengthened the little airline.

"Being attacked was very useful to us. It created a warrior spirit. When people knew that we could be out of business next week, our people went into battle," Herb told me. In other words, the fact that everyone in the company was fighting for the company's survival helped create an environment where innovation thrived. The resulting Innovation Stack has endured for fifty years.

Southwest's Innovation Stack

1. **Maximized Aircraft Utilization.** Herb began with Southwest's central insight: "Planes make money in the air, not on the ground." This might seem obvious until you consider how much time most planes spend on the ground. Southwest made a bet that the more flights it flew, the more profitable the airline would be. There was a point, for example, when Southwest was averaging twice as many flights out of each of its gates as its competitors. How did it manage that?

2. **Ten-Minute Turnaround.** A few years after starting out, financial pressures forced Southwest to sell one of its four airplanes. The airline faced an immediate

problem: how to maintain its schedule with the remaining three planes.

It did what other airlines considered impossible: it started turning planes around in ten minutes or less. From the moment a plane arrived at the gate, passengers disembarked, bags were unloaded, the plane was cleaned and fueled, and the new passengers were boarded, all in ten minutes. Not only did this enable the airline to keep its schedule and accomplish more with fewer airplanes, it also contributed to Southwest's on-time performance, which was soon the best in the industry. But turning around a plane in ten minutes when the industry average was an hour necessitated much more innovation.

3. **Standardized Fleet.** Turning a plane in ten minutes would stress out a Formula 1 pit crew. Baggage off, baggage on, service lavatories, clean the plane, replenish supplies, and perform a dozen FAA-mandated inspections. Southwest simplified these tasks by flying one type of airplane: the Boeing 737. Other carriers averaged ten different types of planes. Southwest's ground, baggage, and maintenance people knew the 737 like a Hell's Angel knows his Harley.

In addition to turnaround speed, flying one kind of plane meant that pilots and crew, who required specialized training on each different plane type, could substitute for each other as needs arose. Southwest was so committed to the 737 that Boeing began building and selling special versions of the 737 just to meet Southwest's needs. Herb told Boeing's CEO, "'We are not going to fly a different airplane, we are going to fly the same airplane with more seats in it.' That was the first time in the history of aviation anybody said that."

4. **Batch Boarding.** Southwest passengers received their plastic, reusable boarding passes as they arrived at the gate, and then boarded on a first come, first served basis. The color-coded boarding passes allowed employees to look at the passengers rather than their tickets, and to welcome them to the flight. Boarding in batches of thirty was also fast. Other airlines boarded in an intricate hierarchy of classes more complex than the seating chart at a royal wedding. This is mind-numbingly slow and inefficient. Southwest chose to treat everyone equally and to treat everyone well.

5. **Open Seating.** Passengers chose their seats when they boarded the plane. This both sped up boarding and simplified reservations. Though somewhat controversial, open seating is actually preferred by Southwest's most profitable passenger—the last-minute business traveler who wants to sit in the front of the aircraft. Herb explained, "We did extensive studies and it kind of amazed us because our business passengers don't want assigned seating. They are the ones that are always making last-minute trips and they say, 'All the good seats are gone.'" But open seating is impossible if the

airline has to enforce rules about who can sit where, so Southwest had to add another component to its Innovation Stack and eliminate such discrimination.

6. **Single Class.** Everyone was equal on a Southwest flight. Having only one class of service decreased boarding time and allowed the company to fit more seats into the plane. Remember, the early growth of Southwest preceded the widespread use of computers, so the benefits of this simplification were even more profound. Other airlines spent massive efforts sorting people into separate lines, lounges, bathrooms, gates, doors, and seats only to ultimately herd them into the same metal tube that arrived all at once.

7. **Fringe Airports.** Turning a plane in ten minutes isn't much use if that same plane has to wait on the tarmac for thirty minutes before receiving takeoff clearance and again before getting to the gate. So Southwest chose airports that were less congested. Want to fly to New York City? Southwest would take you to Islip. Washington, DC? Southwest dropped you in Baltimore with a free bus to the rail station. Some of Southwest's airports were actually closer to downtown areas: Hobby in Houston and Midway in Chicago. Bypassing all that air and ground traffic helped Southwest stay on time, and it was convenient for travelers. Fringe airports also had lower landing fees.

8. **Direct Routes.** Sticking to its goal of keeping its planes in the air, Southwest rejected the hub-and-spoke strategy of most airlines and flew direct. Flying to a hub, then having passengers disembark and get on a plane to their *actual* destination does provide an advantage for airlines: it creates more routes. But airplanes spend more time waiting for arriving flights and transferring passengers, and weather delays at a hub can trash a schedule. Also, putting people on two flights is more expensive than taking them nonstop. By going direct and keeping the planes flying, Southwest kept its ground crews and baggage handlers busy, getting high productivity from both planes and people.

9. **No Food.** Southwest realized that for most passengers, a mediocre airline meal was not a high priority, certainly not when compared to affordable prices and punctuality. Southwest flights averaged only about an hour, so the airline provided peanuts and drinks, and customers were OK with it. For early morning flights, continental breakfasts were available *in the gate area*, a simple solution that saved a tremendous amount of time for the onboard crew.

Even on longer flights, Southwest kept it simple. Herb explained, "We began service between San Antonio and Los Angeles and reduced the round-trip fare by $400. At the press conference a reporter asked, 'That is a long flight—are you going to serve meals?' I said,

'My understanding is that for $400 you can get a pretty good sandwich in Los Angeles.'"

10. **Friendly Staff.** With the possible exception of Con-Air, the nickname given to the federal prison system's maximum-security aircraft, every airline claims to have friendly staff. You as a traveler may find their staff indistinguishably poor, ConAir included. But the people at Southwest were noticeably nicer. To begin with, the company hired only people with great personalities, even if they needed training in their future job function. More important, friendliness was a corporate value and management would go to great lengths to preserve it, including occasionally firing unreasonable customers. Combining naturally friendly people with a culture that placed their needs *before* the customers' or shareholders' energized Southwest's people and made it noticeably more fun to fly.

Southwest supported its people better than any other airline, perhaps any other business. "I was criticized at business schools. They would try to pose a conundrum, 'who comes first, your employees, your customers, or your shareholders?' I would say, wait a second, it is not a conundrum, your employees come first." Herb emphasized his point with a beautiful cumulus formation, then continued. "It is not a big mystery. Employees come first. You treat them well, they treat your customers well, the customers come back, and the shareholders love the results." Have you ever made your boss a heart?

11. **No Stupid Rules.** At a time when other airlines had dozens of tricks to extract the maximum amount of money from each traveler, Southwest's fares made sense. Other carriers embraced such craziness as round trips that cost less than single legs, and two-leg trips that cost less than the first leg alone. Southwest even let you keep the value of your ticket if you had to cancel.

Once Herb saw one of his gate agents trying to help a customer by looking up something in the Southwest rule book, so Herb decided to literally burn the rule book before the whole company. "We had a ceremony to do it," Herb said, fondly recalling the cloud that was once a thousand pages of rules. "We replaced that rule book with guidelines for leaders and the first sentence was, 'Always remember, these are just guidelines and you are free to break them.' We went from a thousand pages of rules to maybe twenty-two of guidelines."

12. **Independent Sales.** Southwest never joined any ticketing system. As a result, if you wanted to fly Southwest, you had to buy your ticket from Southwest. This saved money for the airline and its customers, and over the years it trained passengers to look to Southwest first when they needed to travel.

Herb explained, "We are the only airline that refused to join the global distribution system for selling tickets. If somebody controls your distribution I think they control you. And what is the limit in charging us higher and higher fees as we go forward because we become a captive of theirs?"

13. **Low Prices.** In its quest to make air travel available to those who had previously been unable to afford it, price was Southwest's most important strategy, especially in the early years. The company wanted to square up the airline industry for all those people who "didn't want to fly." Eventually, even the US government had to admit that Southwest was right. A 1993 US Department of Transportation study[71] found that the main reason airline fares were dropping throughout the industry was the low fares offered by Southwest.

SOUTHWEST CHANGED THE airline industry in its first two decades. During a period when nearly every other airline went bankrupt, Southwest was profitable and growing. Almost as amazing as Southwest's early performance is the fact that its founders simply wanted to start a regional airline. They were forced to innovate because the other airlines launched a series of assaults against the start-up, including lawsuits, injunctions, price wars, legislation, and blocked

---

[71] R. Bennett and J. M. Craun (May 1993). "The Airline Deregulation Evolution Continues: The Southwest Effect. Office of Aviation Analysis." US Department of Transportation.

fuel pumps. Southwest was not allowed to copy the existing carriers' way of doing business; it was forced down a different path.

SO IT ALL FIT. Southwest built the most profitable company within the worst industry. There were a dozen cigarette butts in Herb's ashtray when I finally turned off my recorder. But it was after the formal part of our interview concluded that Herb shared perhaps the greatest insight. How much fun it all was!

Fun!

Herb reminded me just how much fun it is doing something new. The team at Southwest had a blast inventing a new way for people to travel. From the baggage handlers to the gate agents to the amazingly friendly folks on the planes, fun was baked into Southwest's culture. The company celebrated every birthday and life event for every employee. It was different from the other airlines, and its people loved that difference.

The fun ran all the way up to the CEO. Herb is fun. In fact, he claimed to be even more fun than I had witnessed. During lunch Herb actually apologized for the fact that he wasn't drinking any alcohol. Herb explained to me that the liver is the only organ in the human body that can regenerate itself, so he always took a month off drinking every year to regrow his liver. And he always did this in February, because it is the shortest month.

Fun matters. Imagine your job is moving luggage off and on an airplane. Does that job seem repetitive and boring? Everyone else in the industry takes a half hour to unload and reload a plane. You and your teammates have been hired to do the job in eight minutes. If you fail, so does the company. Pilots and managers sometimes join you on the tarmac to help, and other times just to marvel at your team's speed. The company that manufactures the plane even listens to your suggestions for improving your job. Imagine being a hero for handling luggage.

Southwest under Herb was a company of heroes, celebrated from the top down. So often I hear businesspeople talk about how hard they work, how the competition is unrelenting, and how people are unreliable. Talking to Herb reminded me how fun it is to be part of a team that is doing something new. When your focus is your customers and not your competitors, it's more fun!

After lunch we drove down Herb Kelleher Way to the Southwest departures area. Six hours of nicotine-enhanced discovery had left my head in the clouds. I've never asked anyone for an autograph, but I was not going to miss a chance with this legend. But I had nothing to write on; every page of my notepad was full. So I grabbed one of the half dozen empty blue boxes of Kool Menthols strewn about Herb's car and asked the man to sign his name. Herb's autograph sits in my study next to my father's slide rule.

A few weeks after our interview, my phone once again rang unexpectedly from a 214 area code. "Jim, I made a mistake signing that pack of Kools for you." Immediately, I

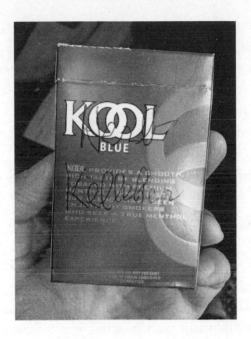

wondered if Herb wanted me to destroy the second-most-prized object in my office. Had the growing wave of anti-smoking political correctness finally reached Herb Time? "Yeah, I only had that ballpoint pen. Next time you're back in Dallas I'll sign you a new one with a black Sharpie." I could picture the cloud from which he spoke.

CHAPTER 12

When

DOES timing affect entrepreneurial success? Absolutely.

That said, I am no master of timing, just another student. My goal for this chapter is to welcome you to class and share a few notes. If you already are a student of the temporal arts, then you can skip to the next chapter and, well, save some time.

Even without mastery, appreciating timing has been hugely helpful, and I began my studies very late. I missed literally hundreds of lessons over three decades before an old Italian man taught me how to appreciate timing with two words.

The Maestro's Lesson

My lamentation that I have never had a mentor is true in my business life, but not in my career as an artist. Every glassblower has a mentor; in fact, we all have the same one: Lino Tagliapietra. Glassblowing is the only profession I know where everyone agrees on who the best practitioner is.

Nobody knows who the best accountant or mortician or loan shark is, but the world's best glassblower is Lino.

Everyone learns from the Maestro, usually by meeting someone who had met someone who had taken one of Lino's classes. Maestro's classes were legendary, right down to an admission process that would impress the Harvard registrar: there was even an essay question, and a collection of T-shirts for sale to salve the pain of rejection.[72] It took me fifteen years to earn a place, but I was finally admitted.

Lino's class lasted two weeks and during that time you were allowed to ask Maestro one question. Each student obsessed over his or her question, and as a result most questions followed the same format: a student would ask Lino how to do something impossible with glass. We would then sit in rapture as Maestro demonstrated how to do it. But when the day came for my question, none of the other students even paid attention to Lino's answer, for my question was so basic that they already knew it. Or so they thought. I asked the best glassblower in the world how to put a simple foot on a bowl.

Putting a foot on a bowl is not complicated; we teach the basic technique in every beginner class. By this point in my career I had performed the process at least a thousand times, but I could never get comfortable with the move. Sometimes it worked and sometimes it didn't. I had studied different techniques, purchased different tools, but nothing worked consistently. Sometimes the foot would proudly elevate the piece on top; other times it looked like it had

---

[72] The most popular says simply, "Because that's how Lino does it."

Putting a foot on a bowl.

frozen while trying to escape. Every time I needed to apply a foot, I got anxious. So, after fifteen years of stress and failure, I used my one question to ask the Maestro how to do this right.

I expected him to answer me as he had the other students, by demonstrating the proper technique, but that is not what Maestro did. Lino told me to make a bowl, which I did promptly. Then he told me to make a foot, which is simply a hot gather of glass taken directly from the furnace and shaped into a tennis ball–sized glob. I made the foot.

He then told me to put the foot on the bowl, but just as I

was about to let the hot foot drop onto the colder bowl, he said: *Wait*. I stood there with the bowl in my left hand and the foot in my right until he gave the second half of the lesson: *Now*. I let the now-slightly-less-hot foot fall and it went on perfectly. This blew my mind.

I was expecting a lesson in *how*, but Lino gave me a lesson in *when*. I already knew *how*—I had been doing the *how* part right for fifteen years. My problem was *when*. If you make a shape out of glass that is too hot, you can make the shape, but the glass will just collapse afterward. If the glass is too cold, however, it becomes too stiff and you cannot make the shape in the first place. It's timing, not technique.

I left the studio that evening thinking about all the other places in my life where I had done the right thing at the wrong time. How many times had I spoken when the other person was not ready to listen? How often had I been too late or too early with the right answer? I saw a cascade of failures over my lifetime resulting from knowing *how* to do something, but ignoring *when* to do it. I decided to become a student of *when*.

Learning When

Schools teach *how*. We learn to copy what works with the emphasis always on the *how* and not the *when*. I learned how to construct complicated mathematical models, but never learned when presenting such a model was inappropriate. I learned to reason logically, but never learned when logic might offend someone. I learned contract law, but never learned when to just shake hands.

It is difficult to fault our schools for emphasizing *how*, since it is difficult to study *when*. Determining how to perform a task means repeating the steps over and over until you achieve a successful result. Once we learn how to do something, the formal learning usually stops. We then learn how to do the next thing.

Learning *when* to do something is far more difficult than learning *how* to do that same thing, if only because we must always learn *how* first. We must begin by learning how to do a task so well that we can do it correctly every time. Then, and only then, can we perform this task at various times and see if the results change depending on when we perform it.

Unless your task is one that can be done in the laboratory, the sheer volume of variables is overwhelming. I witnessed this firsthand when I took my first course in econometrics. Econometrics is where eager young economists learn why their profession is called the Dismal Science. Basically, we learned a bunch of math that allowed us to take a given set of historical data and project future behaviors. I poured myself into the intricate math of a dozen different predictive techniques that would give me the power to see the future. But since each technique predicted a different future state, the true secret was knowing when to use a particular tool. The professor finally admitted at the end of the course that nobody knew when. The math worked great, but the smartest minds in economics could not determine when to use any particular technique over another. The only accurate prediction I made as a result of that class was that I would no longer study econometrics.

It is not just economists who fail to learn *when*; most attempts to study timing become overwhelmingly complex. Do not despair. Our goal here is not to derive some formula for perfect timing, but to learn to recognize some patterns that can help us when opportunities arise. Indeed, in my study of entrepreneurial companies, several patterns kept reappearing.

Simplifying Time

Instead of trying to see time as an overwhelmingly infinite set of temporal options, I find it easier to just ask, "When should we begin?" There are really only two answers to this question: now or later.[73] Now is often the right answer. In this world of highly similar products, speed is a huge advantage. If you create innovation first, economics tells us that you can profit from it only until your competitors copy you. And there is good reason to believe that you won't have much time. The history of simultaneous innovation also suggests that someone else has had the same idea, so again the reward goes to the first mover.

In fact, *now* is so often the right answer that many successful people default to answering the question *When should we begin?* by always saying *Now!* (And, yes, that answer usually includes an exclamation point.) They always want to be first, but it really depends on the race.

---

[73] The past, as we often lament, is no longer a viable option.

First Failures

If you are racing through the streets of Europe, the type of race matters. Formula 1 drivers in Monaco wind through such narrow streets that there are very few opportunities to pass. The car in the pole position usually wins the race. But in a bicycle race through those same streets, the leader will often become exhausted before the race is finished, handing victory to those who waited patiently in the slipstream.

In the world of entrepreneurship, being first is not always best. This is because some elements of the Innovation Stack depend on each other. When a critical element is outside your control, waiting can be the best option. It's possible to launch world-changing technology too early.

Do you recall the first social network? Wrong, it was GeoCities back in 1995. Friendster came next in 2002 and did better. Then MySpace elbowed out Friendster beginning in 2003. Finally, Facebook took over. Why are we not all connecting with each other over Geo-chat? Part of the answer is that GeoCities, Friendster, and MySpace all launched before mobile computing was commonplace. Without always-on access to the system, the appeal of a social network is diminished, and before mobile phones we weren't always carrying cameras.

Should we fault GeoCities, Friendster, and MySpace for not anticipating the looming ubiquity of mobile devices? Each of those companies was OK for its time, but Facebook's timing was fantastic. Facebook had a dozen components of its Innovation Stack ready when mobile exploded, and then it quickly purchased Instagram when Instagram was beating it in mobile.

You can be too early. Quick, name the eighteenth search engine company to launch.[74]

The Missing Element

Sometimes a key element of an Innovation Stack is missing. The market for ride sharing provides a great example. The idea of ride sharing has been around for at least forty years. I took my first ride share in Leningrad in 1986 while traveling around the Soviet Union aggressively bartering off a bunch of baggy stonewashed denim.[75] I soon learned that Leningrad residents treated any single-passenger vehicle as a potential taxicab. You could hail any car that had just a driver in it and arrange transportation across town at any time.

The system was fantastic! A driver who didn't already have other passengers in the car would stop and pick up any random stranger standing on the edge of the roadway with his or her hand raised. Rides were cheap, plentiful, and safe.

Safety was key. One of the worst things about ride sharing is the creepiness of getting into a stranger's car, or letting a stranger into your car. Ride sharing when I was young

---

[74] You might want to Google that.
[75] The only Russian phrase I knew translated as "The thirty pairs of blue jeans are for my personal use."

was called *hitchhiking*, and every kid learned it was dangerous for both the driver and the passenger.

The Soviet Union had many problems, but violent crime was not one of them. If you owned a car in the USSR the government knew who you were, and you knew that it knew. In fact, it knew so much about everybody that people felt safe and the whole ride-sharing thing worked. But it only worked over there.

I'm sure that several thousand people realized how great it would be to bring such a system to the United States, but the timing would not be right for several decades. Ride sharing in this country would be impossible until we solved the safety problem. We needed to wait for mobile phones with their identity systems, moving maps, stranger ratings, and cashless payments. Thirty years later, I can finally use ride sharing in the United States, and many of the drivers still speak Russian.

A MISSING ELEMENT can doom an Innovation Stack. In ride sharing, the missing innovation was in the area of safety. It doesn't matter how great the other components of an Innovation Stack are, if a necessary component is missing, you must wait to innovate. Our Innovation Stack at Square had a missing component for our first year, which we discovered the first day: the credit card networks had rules specifically prohibiting what we were doing. The moment described in chapter 3 when Mastercard agreed to change its rules was a critical point in the birth of our company. Without that rule change, the other dozen things we were doing would have been irrelevant. But we were not just going to do nothing in the meantime.

The Way to Wait

If you are purposely waiting for an element of your Innovation Stack to be ready, is there anything to do in the meantime? Yes. The decision to wait implies that at some future time you will have to move, so you still have plenty to do. You work on all the other elements of your Innovation Stack so that when the final element exists everything else is ready to go. This is risky.

For example, there was no guarantee that Mastercard and Visa would change their rules. In the year it took to get them to agree, we worked on other elements of our Innovation Stack with the hope that the last piece would eventually happen. It was a gamble, for we had no guarantee that the card networks would see it our way. At Square, we worked feverishly for when that time came. When it did, the rest of our Stack was ready to go and the gamble paid off.

Of course, building the rest of your Innovation Stack while a critical element is missing depends on how critical that missing element is to your operations. I believe that it was OK for Square to initially violate those seventeen rules and regulations as we built our system. If things went bad at Square, we could just shut down our system, and Jack and I could reimburse anyone who lost money. Moving a few thousand dollars around before we got approval to launch was quite different from the situation Herb and the team at Southwest faced.

Southwest could not even taxi a plane to a runway without federal permission, so they had to wait. Training ground crew to turn a plane in ten minutes would be nearly impossible without real passengers, real luggage, and a real plane. Southwest could not just start flying and hope the regulators saw it their way.

But in general, the sooner you can build the various elements of your Innovation Stack, the longer those elements have time to adjust to each other and evolve. Waiting for one element should not impede all the others. Of course, this is risky, but most of the entrepreneurs I studied all took this same type of risk, even if it made them uncomfortable.

Right Feels Early

One of my favorite quotations from A. P. Giannini was a confession he made to his lawyers: "It makes me sick and tired to hear what I can't do. If I know I'm right and can justify myself, I go ahead, I take a chance."[76] This quotation captures the attitude of most of the entrepreneurs I have met and studied: the willingness to accept uncertainty as they move forward.

So how does this feel? Well, in my case I get nervous. Toward the end of my first year at Square I was actually having "mild" panic attacks about all our unresolved issues. I remember pulling off the road one day and running into a

---

[76] *The Saturday Evening Post*, December 4, 1947, p. 133.

pharmacy and getting a bottle of aspirin to fight the heart attack I was sure I was having. *Right* feels early.

If the timing feels right, you are probably too late. As we learned in chapter 6, the time humans feel *right* is when we are in sync with the rest of the herd. So if the innovation feels right, it probably feels right to a hundred other people with the same idea. If it feels too early, in my experience, that's a good time to leave the walled city. There is no way to know when the unknown is arriving, but it will probably arrive sooner than you think.

The Horizon of Possibility

Think of the world as a series of interdependent Innovation Stacks. Somebody else's new invention may be the missing piece to your Innovation Stack. Every day you get a new set of tools. I call this the Horizon of Possibility. Just beyond what we can see, there are things happening that help our cause.

For instance, the mobile phone has made other innovation possible. When Jack and I launched Square, the only thing we knew was that mobile technology was going to change everything, which is why we hired an iPhone programmer before knowing what the company would actually do.

In other words, we bet on mobile technology changing the world back in 2009, before it happened. We had no idea what those changes would look like, but we prepared as well as we could and worked on a problem whose solution required many new inventions. Some of those inventions were ours, but most came from a world that was also adapting and evolving.

Change and innovation occur at constantly increasing rates. Once we become used to a rate of change, we are already thinking too slowly. Most of this change is beyond our comprehension or control, but not all.

Innovation Stack–Driven Change

The actions of an entrepreneurial firm can actually drive change, sometimes supplying that missing element. In other words, leaping can cause you to grow wings.

In Square's case, our big missing element was permission from the card networks. We actively pursued this change, aided by a system that was already fully functional, if not legal. Had we not already built the system, Mastercard and Visa probably never would have bothered to rewrite their rules. Even if they had, they might have written the new rules in a way that would still prevent Square from functioning as it did. Our system gave them something to aim for. Once Mastercard agreed to revise its regulations, the tone of our conversations was basically, "Square is cool, so how do we make it compliant?"

The seminal event in Southwest's climb to become the nation's top airline was federal deregulation of the airlines, an event that happened seven years after Southwest began flying. According to Herb, "Southwest Airlines was the focus of federal deregulation because of what we had accomplished. Senator Kennedy called and said, 'Why does it cost a hell of a lot more to fly from Boston to New York than from Dallas to Houston?' and we said, 'Because we are not regulated by the federal government.'" As a Texas-only airline, Southwest was able to avoid federal price regulation. With its demonstrably better price, speed, and service, it was the main example Senator Kennedy cited to support airline deregulation. In other words, Southwest's Innovation Stack spawned an additional element, an element that would allow Southwest to become the nation's largest airline. If it could grow fast enough.

Being Ready

An important part of timing is being ready when the missing elements suddenly appear. I have seen the following pattern in dozens of entrepreneurial companies: the Innovation Stack begins to function, and then the world suddenly changes; but because the Innovation Stack is still evolving, the company can quickly capitalize on this new world order before any other firm can adapt to the new ecosystem.

At the time of deregulation in 1978, Southwest Airlines had already been flying passengers around for seven years as a small regional airline. But because of its earlier battles with the airlines and regulators, Southwest's flights, planes, finances, pricing, staff, pilots, passengers, and a dozen other blocks in its Innovation Stack were ready before deregulation hit. When the change came, Southwest was already in the air doing five hundred knots, the only company prepared for this new world. It had built an Innovation Stack that allowed it to have happier customers, lower fares, better punctuality, and better safety within Texas; now it just had to scale everything up. Equally important was Southwest's culture, which was accustomed to adapting quickly.

Bank of America was ready for a form of deregulation that could not come fast enough for A. P. Giannini. His bank had a well-developed Innovation Stack in California that allowed it to profitably serve the needs of individuals and small businesses, but was prevented from growing by state and federal laws restricting both branch and interstate banking. A.P. threw himself into politics to remove those barriers, and as each was lifted, Bank of America was ready.

We at Square had our Innovation Stack running when Steve Jobs again surprised the world. We had no idea what was coming. The only thing we knew was that Apple wanted us to build a secure, windowless room and sign a bunch of strongly worded legal documents. A team came out to inspect our makeshift vault and ensure that they could chain down whatever they might later deliver. Only six of us were ever allowed in that room, and we're still not allowed to discuss anything that might have happened in there.

But what the public does know is that when Steve Jobs showed the world the first iPad, Square was the only financial application on it. That first product has today become our flagship product, anchoring an ecosystem of tools for running whole businesses. The iPad allowed Square to build an entirely new seller ecosystem, and we had no idea it was coming.

This is the pattern for explosive growth. An entrepreneurial company has a working Innovation Stack when some external market change happens. The new change supercharges the Innovation Stack, which quickly adapts and creates new synergies. While we cannot precisely model how the interrelationships work, we can see the pattern. We can also see the world-changing results, and feel the pressure of a new temporal burden.

Time to Grow

There is a time when the answer to *when* is always *now!* Once an Innovation Stack is complete and expanding the market to new customers, it is time to grow. And grow fast!

In Square's case, once our Innovation Stack was working we had a massive demand that we had to meet. Fortunately, most of our innovation optimized the company for speed and growth, so we could go from zero to two million customers without having to distort the space-time continuum. Not that it wasn't stressful—by any measure a company that doubles in size every other month is a pressure cooker. But there is really no choice. You have to grow to meet the market demand or risk losing everything.

It is very difficult to displace a company with an Innovation Stack in a market where it is moving superfast. When Amazon tried to copy Square, it was still easier to become a Square customer than an Amazon customer. In other words, there was no massive line of people outside our door waiting to get in.

Long Lines Are Dangerous

If the line gets too long, watch out. An Innovation Stack cannot protect your company in markets you ignore. Quite the opposite—the success of your Innovation Stack creates a strong incentive for copycats to take your Stack and apply it someplace that you are neglecting. Without you as a competitor, they may just succeed.

In Square's case, a company called iZettle in Sweden copied everything it could from Square's Innovation Stack and then added several elements of its own. Since we had no product outside the United States, it had the market to itself and was able to build a very successful copycat.

In Southwest's case, it let a giant line form across the Brooklyn Bridge. The closest Southwest came to New York was Islip, way out on Long Island. It kept the nation's busiest travel market waiting for discount air travel for thirty-one years. Meanwhile, in 1999, JetBlue was able to get seventy-five takeoff/landing slots at JFK Airport and had the market to itself for a decade, long enough to build its own Innovation Stack. JetBlue was the only Southwest competitor that launched during Herb's tenure and survived. In some ways, JetBlue has now taken the lead in low-cost air travel, as we'll see in chapter 15 on pricing.

NOT EVEN THE world's best econometrician knows exactly when to make a move. Experience helps, but by definition it is impossible to have experience for anything that is truly new. I find, however, that simply being aware of the temporal components makes my enterprises more nimble. I race to be ready early. But as soon as I feel ready a voice in my head with a strong Italian accent asks, *"Is the world also ready?"*

If the world is ready, then creating an Innovation Stack comes with a responsibility to create a market for as many new customers as possible. You are rewarded with a massive market that is nearly impossible for competitors to steal, so long as you can grow fast enough. This is fun, stressful, and necessary work.

This massive growth also has an effect on the market that is far different from what people believe.

PART 3

INNOVATION PHYSICS

WE HAVE NOW examined four companies that fit a pattern. Entrepreneurs set out to solve a perfect problem, but since they cannot copy the solution, they are forced down a path of invention. The resulting Innovation Stack expands the market to include many people who could not previously participate (have a bank account, buy new furniture, travel by plane, or accept credit cards).

Now that you've witnessed this pattern, you may begin to notice it all around you. Innovation Stacks tend to evolve out of sight, concealed within tiny firms that will someday become giants. Finding an entrepreneurial company at this early stage is like discovering an invasive plant species when it is just a seed stuck to someone's shoe. Once the Stack forms and the company grows, it becomes more visible.

Even easier to find, if you are willing to mine the past, are Innovation Stacks from decades or centuries ago that have now become their own markets. Automobiles and frozen foods are great examples, but there are thousands more. For instance, the main reason that the Bank of Italy (now Bank of America) example doesn't seem more radical is that almost every major bank has copied Bank of Italy—it just took a hundred years. Look back and see the Stack.

There is a cost to learning from the past, however, because history trades drama for data. Summarizing the results of some ancient battle makes the terror of war seem like a game of chess. But the drama is important to understand because entrepreneurship is a battle, not a book. And your odds don't look good.

The sheer volume of unknown and sometimes unknowable aspects of a new market clouds every view. Advice from "experts" in similar markets can be comically incorrect.[77] You simply cannot study something that doesn't exist. The journey into the unknown is made without a map.

You are blind.

The lack of reliable forecasting not only clouds your vision, it also frightens investors. While investors do look for a return *on* capital, they are more concerned with the return *of* capital. Presenting a map with dragons drawn at the end of a flat earth is no way to get a boat loan. At Square, Jack and I didn't even bother courting investors until we had a working product, a functional team, and happy customers. Even if you can gather some resources, you will never have as many as those businesses within the city walls.

You are blind and poor.

It isn't just investors who get spooked; the lack of familiarity frightens potential partners as well. Explaining something truly new is incredibly difficult. Square was a simple idea, but Jack and I were amazed by how hard it was to explain before

---

[77] The first two payment industry experts we worked with at Square gave us advice that was so bad it was almost good. We simply did the opposite of what they recommended. And we stopped working with "experts."

we had a working prototype. If you cannot draw an analogy from an existing product, then most people will never understand it. As a result, you cannot partner with other companies and are lucky to be able to gather even a small team of believers.

You are blind and poor and alone.

Well, you're not *entirely* alone. The other businesses already working in similar markets will, sooner or later, see your moves as a threat. Square was never a threat to Visa, but Visa still had a plan for putting us out of business.[78] They will attack you every way they can. They will attack from their established positions or the press or the courts. If these attacks fail, they might even pass new laws to protect themselves. Even if your ultimate intention is to expand the market to people the incumbents are currently ignoring, there will be war.

You are blind and poor and alone and hunted.

There is, however, something powerful that protects you: a different set of rules. This new entrepreneurial world inverts some of the normal rules of business. Customers become coworkers, low price ensures profits, massive growth doesn't displace competitors, and you repel attacks by "doing nothing." I know this sounds strange.

It's like quantum mechanics versus classical physics. Both systems have the concept of energy, but in daily life the quantum explanation of energy is rarely necessary. In fact,

---

[78] I learned, from a former Visa executive looking for a job, about a three-ring binder containing a strategy on how Visa could kill Square. I never saw the binder.

even using quantum mechanics as an analogy is odd, because unless you're a physicist you likely have no idea what quantum mechanics is. Which is my point. Billions of people live their lives with no concept of perturbation theory or eigenstates.[79] Classical physics explains daily life; the situations when understanding the world requires quantum mechanics are so rare you can just avoid them. But those few who do understand quantum mechanics enable us to build computers a million times more powerful.

So it is with entrepreneurship. You don't need to understand perfect problems or messy Innovation Stacks. You can spend most of your life, as I did, thinking that invention is incremental and that the explosive change is just luck. The few times when entrepreneurship is required are so rare you can avoid them. But understanding entrepreneurship enables us to build solutions for millions of people.

Even for scientists, quantum mechanics is weird. They are eternally hypothesizing and experimenting; but while this understanding evolves, the first quantum computers are already being built. Likewise, the world of entrepreneurship is still poorly understood, but that should not stop us from harnessing some of its unique powers.

---

[79] Sorry, I can't explain these things since I'm not a physicist. I do, however, deeply respect your optimism.

CHAPTER 13

Stack Attack

S OMETIMES pictures lie. Grow-
ing up in St. Louis, Missouri, under the shadow of the Gate-
way Arch, every kid learned the stories of how the pioneers
settled the West. Images of peaceful wagon trains and
happy Caucasians in coonskin hats made a person long to
follow the sunset and claim their forty acres. In fact, most of
those paintings were made in New England, probably by
people who just wanted their neighbors to leave. The real
settlers didn't carry easels and paint. People who intentionally burned down their houses to reclaim the nails before
moving farther west weren't toting tubes of burnt sienna.
Life on the frontier could be deadly.

The fact that a company is expanding a market, and claim-
ing previously unclaimed territory, does not mean this expansion will be peaceful. In every industry where I studied an
entrepreneur, there was scorched earth. There is always a war.

Entrepreneurial companies get attacked. And by attacked, I mean something beyond normal competition. I'm

talking about a level of ferocity that could end with a trial at The Hague. Once they notice you, they try to wipe you off the planet. So, we had better learn how to fight.

Charred Ground

Southwest Airlines began life in a courtroom. Herb Kelleher was not even an airline executive in the earliest days; he was the attorney fighting for Southwest. Herb and SWA won, but the other airlines took the case all the way to both the Texas and the US Supreme Courts. Even after winning in these courts, Southwest found more obstacles on the runway. Before the first Southwest flight ever took off, other airlines pressured the underwriters to withdraw from Southwest's IPO and obtained a restraining order forbidding Southwest from beginning service.

IKEA's early competitors banded together to boycott any manufacturers who worked with the young company, and they got the trade association to ban IKEA from the furniture mart. They banned Kamprad personally from the trade events and unleashed brutal personal and political attacks.

Dozens of companies attacked Square. One of these was the very company whose CEO called me an idiot for trying to serve small merchants. It launched a negative PR campaign against us, including a video from the CEO that talked about a glassblower stealing your credit card data. We really didn't pay much attention to these attacks, until the day we were targeted by the most dangerous company on the planet.

Amazon's Aftermath

I opened this book with Square's first brush with Amazon. I explained what happened but not why it worked. To attribute the outcome to simple good luck or some other irreproducible irregularity avoids two critical questions: *Was our survival more than just luck?* and *Could what saved Square save other companies?* Yes and yes.

Southwest Airlines should have died from the onslaught of the major airlines and the blocked fuel hydrants. IKEA should have died from the boycott or the banishment. Bank of Italy should have succumbed to the attacks of the eastern banks or the government regulators. All of these companies, while they were still small, were viciously assaulted. They not only survived, but became the largest and most powerful firms in their respective industries. This wasn't luck.

The Math of an Attack

An Innovation Stack isn't simply a list of independent changes to an existing business model. The innovation is integrated. Each block in the Stack only works in conjunction with all the others, and the entire Stack fails if one block is missing. For example, regarding Square's Innovation Stack, online sign-up is great, but it only really works if you dispense with traditional FICO underwriting, and you can only do that if you've developed new ways to model risk, and you can only develop those models with high volume, which necessitates a number of the other blocks in the

Stack. Copying just one—or even a few—of our elements wasn't going to be enough for our competition to beat us. Amazon would have to copy them all successfully in order to win. And the math involved in doing that gets very tricky.

So far, we have examined fourteen elements of Square's Innovation Stack. Let's say that a company has a 75 percent chance of copying any one element successfully. Since the company in our example is Amazon, let's give it an 80 percent shot at getting each one right. So, with one element, it's at 80 percent. To get two elements right, it's got a 64 percent chance. And only a 51 percent chance of copying three correctly, a 41 percent chance of copying four, and a 33 percent chance at successfully copying five of the elements we were utilizing every day. You see where this is going. Even a place with all the talent and resources of Amazon can't escape math. Its chances of copying all fourteen of our elements (0.8^{14}) were about 4 percent. Which was still scary, but no reason to order diapers.

This is admittedly an oversimplified view, because it assumes that each element in an Innovation Stack is independent, but in reality, each element is tied to the others. The complexities of the impact that fourteen innovative elements have when simultaneously unleashed on an industry are compounded by the interrelationships of those elements themselves. When everything affects everything, you have a *dynamic system*. Dynamic systems are hard to understand and nearly impossible to copy.

To understand a dynamic system, imagine a jump rope. Let's first consider the mass of the rope itself—it cannot be too heavy or too light. For instance, if you try to jump a piece of thread, you can't get it spinning because a piece of thread doesn't weigh enough. In other words, the mass of the rope affects the rotation of the rope, which affects the shape of the rope. That's why you can't jump a thread.

Now let's add another variable, elasticity. If the rope is a yellow bungee cord, which will elongate as tension is applied, the speed of the rotation of the rope will now change its length. And a changing length affects the speed of rotation and the mass per unit of length. Confused yet? You probably should be.

We humans are no good at modeling more than a couple of variables simultaneously. The math quickly becomes overwhelming. If you have two variables that affect each other, you have one possible interaction. If you have eight variables, there are 251,548,592 possible interactions.[80] In other words, you're never going to model an Innovation Stack on a spreadsheet—you can't do the math.

But companies love math, especially math that senior managers can use to make decisions. Take that math away, and they are left with nothing concrete upon which to base a decision. So where does all this complexity leave our entrepreneur? Actually, in a really good place.

Innovation Interlock

Entrepreneurs fighting for survival outside the civilized market don't build mathematical models of what will happen,

---

[80] The number of distinct connected labeled graphs with n nodes. In other words, a system where everything influences everything else.

they just do it and observe. Jumping rope with a bungee cord isn't impossible; you try, experience what happens, and make adjustments. The effects of each element on the other elements, while impossible to predict, are relatively easy to observe and respond to.

And because these companies are start-ups when they develop their Innovation Stacks, adapting in response to the interrelationships of stacked innovation is relatively easy—small companies are quick to change. So the changes get made, which necessitates other changes, and then the organization changes again. This cycle repeats and repeats, and with each iteration, each element of the Stack adapts to all its neighbors.

In other words, you cannot view the elements of an Innovation Stack individually. The innovation evolves as a whole. No single element can be inserted or removed without changing the behavior of the other elements.

For instance, if another airline asked its pilots to clean the cabin, but didn't have the pressure to turn the plane around in ten minutes and the baggage handlers racing like a Formula 1 pit crew, the pilots might become resentful, since this is not normally what pilots are expected to do. But at Southwest, the entire culture supported a fast turnaround, so the pilots dived for diapers in the seatback pockets.

Even without mathematical certainty, it makes intuitive sense. At Square, much of our innovation was the direct result of other innovation. For instance, because we designed such incredibly inexpensive hardware, we were able to offer free sign-up and no-fee cancellations.

Because we welcomed people who had never processed credit cards before, many of whom had no credit history, we had to develop our own fraud detection systems. But those systems were built without the credit bureaus, so they evolved in their own way. After a few million iterations, we now have a finely tuned system that is impossible to copy. Not that competitors don't try.

Ted Is Dead

Remember Ted? Ted was actually the name of a discount airline launched by United in 2004. People said that *Ted* stood for "the end of *United*" or "*United* without You 'n' I on board." United killed Ted in 2008, but not before it set a longevity record as the most successful effort of a major airline to copy Southwest. Delta launched Song, which went off-key after only three years. Continental Lite also had tailwinds to the graveyard.

But these companies, United, Continental,[81] and Delta, were the top survivors of a ruthlessly competitive airline industry—an industry where paint remover is a line item on corporate budgets. These larger, more experienced companies seemingly should have had no problems copying a start-up. So why didn't Ted succeed?

Before launching Ted, United studied Southwest for over thirty years, so it certainly knew what Southwest was doing. Furthermore, United had inside knowledge of the

---

[81] I know, but it was alive at the time.

airline business and was the nation's second-biggest carrier. It copied several parts of Southwest's Innovation Stack. Ted removed the meal service, offered low fares, standardized by using fuel-efficient Airbus A320s, and even tried to create a recognizably quirky brand identity. But it couldn't replicate even half of Southwest's innovation.

Ted kept two classes of service, which necessitated different reservation and boarding systems. It retained assigned seats. It used United pilots, who had different contracts and had to have training on the A320s as well as on other United aircraft. It had fewer planes in its fleet, so it could not match Southwest's frequency of service. Ted was a discount airline the way a black cat with a white stripe down its back is a skunk. Herb Kelleher told me why no competitor could replicate Southwest's Innovation Stack: "They all took one thing out of twenty and said, 'This is what is going to make us the next Southwest,' but actually it was our holistic mixture."

The copycats also forget that corporate culture is itself part of an Innovation Stack. A corporate culture that evolves along with the Innovation Stack naturally harmonizes with and helps create the innovation. Southwest had developed its Innovation Stack by surviving in the marketplace. Everything about Southwest's culture supported its Innovation Stack. Ted and the other doomed copycats tried to impose a culture and set of business practices as a management exercise with all the sincerity of a telemarketer telling you to "have a nice day."

Ted's dead.

No Reaction Necessary

Doing nothing, now that's really something. How could any reasonable leader watch a competitor attacking his or her company and decide to do nothing?

The decision to not respond to a direct competitive threat is either outrageous or natural, depending on the focus. If your focus is on your competitors, to ignore an attack would be outrageous. Many companies in established industries study their competitors more closely than they study their customers. This makes sense. In an industry that is growing slowly through incremental innovation, copying is actually a sound strategy. In fact, copying one's competitors makes sense even outside the business world.

Perhaps the greatest loss in sports history was when the American sailing team lost to Australia in the 1983 America's Cup. America had successfully defended the cup for 132 years, recorded history's longest winning streak. The Australians had two advantages in the race: a novel "winged keel" that made everyone wonder if their boat was faster, and some awesome tunes from Men at Work that made everyone wonder what a Vegemite sandwich was. Real sailors, however, know that the actual reason Australia won was because the Americans broke the cardinal rule of sailing: *copy your competition.*

Copying in sailing goes by the name *covering*, and the concept is simple. If you have a lead over your opponents and they turn one direction, you must turn the same direction. Basically, you don't want your opponents to catch some wind that you miss. If you zig while they zag you may spend the rest of your life weeping to the tune of "Down Under."

In the seventh and deciding race of the competition, the Americans had a commanding lead over the Aussie boat. The Americans' lead was so great, they chose not to cover. The Aussies sailed the other direction, caught a better wind, and passed the Americans. The American boat then tacked back and forth fifty times trying to get the Aussies to make the same mistake. But the Australians copied every turn the Americans made and eventually someone at the New York Yacht Club had to find the keys to a trophy case that had been locked since Millard Fillmore's administration.

In a stable and established market, companies all zig and zag together. Coke copies Pepsi, Microsoft copies Google, NBC copies ABC, it just makes sense.

But what if, like Columbus, you are more concerned about sailing off the edge of the known world than about the ship behind you? A company that creates its own Innovation Stack does not do so by copying innovation. Innovation Stacks evolve from a focus on the customer, usually a customer new to the market. As the company matures, there is so much new feedback from a growing base of customers that the company has an ever-expanding list of things to do.

Customer Focus

So the question is, if a competitor attacks an entrepreneurial company, should that company focus on the attacking competitor or on its own customers? Keep in mind that most of these customers were not stolen from the attacking competitor, but are totally new to the market. Giannini gave banking services to people who had never used a bank. Southwest took more traffic away from the bus lines than the airlines. Most of Square's customers had never processed credit cards before. It made sense to focus on—and listen to—these new customers, especially since nobody else was.

And so we see a critical difference between an entrepreneurial company and a regular business in its response to an attack. In response to a competitive threat, the regular business should respond to (copy) what the competition does. The entrepreneurial company, in contrast, should maintain the focus on its customers and not change too much in the face of even a direct attack. If it does choose to respond, the entrepreneurial company can use its Innovation Stack as a weapon. Southwest's $13 fare war is a great example.

In 1973, Braniff cut its fare between Dallas and Houston to $13, half of what Southwest charged. The Dallas–Houston run was Southwest's primary source of profit—competing at that rate, even with its Innovation Stack and greater cost efficiency, would be disastrous. Braniff's pricing attack violated US antitrust law, but the executives hoped to drive Southwest out of business before Herb could take them to court. Winning in court wouldn't matter if Southwest was dead, so Herb needed a fast solution. He and his team devised a plan by looking at their customers.

Southwest knew that most of the passengers on the Dallas–Houston route were businesspeople. These businesspeople flew Southwest primarily for the convenience of multiple flights, easy changes, open seating, and on-time performance. Braniff could set any price it wanted, but it could not replicate the other effects of Southwest's Innovation Stack. These business fliers were not choosing Southwest simply because of the low price, a price their employers reimbursed them for anyway.

So Southwest offered fliers the option of paying only $13, or they could pay the full fare of $26 and get a complimentary bottle of Chivas Regal scotch, Crown Royal whiskey, or Smirnoff vodka. Most of the passengers stayed with Southwest and chose to pay the full fare and get the booze. Southwest managed to outsell Braniff at twice the price, and for the length of that promotion became the largest liquor distributor in Texas.

While Braniff was watching Southwest, Southwest was watching its customers. Planes don't have rearview mirrors, and neither do great entrepreneurial companies. They focus on their customers and on the Innovation Stack that serves those customers. Even if they didn't know they had one until now. An entrepreneurial firm, in response to a competitive attack, may appear to be doing nothing, but it may simply be doing *nothing different.*

As a child, I was once advised by an adult, "Don't fight back and the bullies will leave you alone." That was terrible advice at the time, but the logic may now apply. The peculiar math of an Innovation Stack can protect your organization even if you do "nothing." If you are doing everything you can for your customers and company, then ignoring competitive attacks can be sound advice. And besides, you may have millions of allies.

CHAPTER 14

The Invisible Army

B EING attacked by a much larger competitor, or an entire industry of competitors, feels scary and very lonely. When Amazon first attacked Square I tried to find any other companies in our situation. I wanted to copy their solutions, or at least learn from their mistakes. I failed. But it turned out that we were not alone, I was just looking for the wrong type of company.

Entrepreneurial companies are surrounded by millions of potential customers who are outside the wall as well. In every case where I saw a company forge an Innovation Stack, there were millions of new customers eagerly waiting for a product they never knew existed.

These customers are difficult to see at first, especially if you view the world from within the walled city. When Southwest was beginning, the prevailing wisdom was that people didn't actually want to fly, and the US government had data supporting this absurd assertion. Of course, the government was surveying people on planes while most of Southwest's future customers were on the Dirty Dog.[82]

This is not surprising, because measurements are based on what's measurable. When the government began keeping records on air travel, it counted only people who flew on airplanes: mostly business fliers and rich folks. If you survey only the wealthy, you might conclude that polo is a much more popular sport than it actually is. But this bias isn't always the fault of the survey makers, it is simply the nature of the new. Until something exists, it is not going to appear in any graph.

Herb and the team at Southwest looked at the statistics differently. "The government estimated that between 15 and 20 percent of adults in America had never flown on a single commercial flight," he told me. "That sounds like a pretty big market opportunity, doesn't it?" Indeed it was.

Most Square customers were tiny businesses that had never been able to accept credit cards. Most IKEA customers had never purchased new furniture. Most Bank of Italy customers had never been into a bank. And none of these people ever appeared as a statistic until the industry expanded to include them. Invisible does not mean uninterested. Invisible markets can be massive, but it is nearly impossible to prove that beforehand because all the measurements are optimized for the current market.

---

[82] What riders called traveling on Greyhound buses.

Adopters and Adapters

Customers new to a market hold few preconceptions, which is one of the great benefits of massively expanding an industry through innovation. Your new customers learn how to participate in the market from *your way* of doing business. This is a powerful advantage that influences both your Innovation Stack and your competitive position. The first group of customers are traditionally called *early adopters*, but in the world of Innovation Stacks calling them *early adapters* is more accurate. In fact, some innovation is only possible if new, adaptable customers board in a group, assemble their own furniture, and swipe through the wobble.

When we began Square, the majority of our customers had never before accepted credit cards. We taught them to expect simple, low rates. We taught them to operate without live customer support. We taught them to expect settlement three days faster than the industry average, and to expect not to pay transaction fees, chargeback fees, or cancellation fees. We taught them to reject a multiyear contract. We taught them to expect free hardware and beautiful software.

Southwest taught its customers to board in groups and to choose their own seats on the plane. Its customers got used to eating before the flight and not changing planes in some hub. They expected not to pay baggage fees or cancellation penalties. Southwest eventually even taught its customers to use Southwest.com by keeping its fares off all other websites. The Southwest passenger's expectations are exactly what Southwest delivers, because Southwest custom built its market.

Herb explained, "In essence, we are training people to be Southwest customers. One of the biggest complaints that we had on an ongoing basis was not having assigned seats. And I understand because everybody likes to think, 'My little nest is waiting for me.'" But Southwest's customers value the flight more than the nest.

IKEA taught customers to visit a massive showroom and choose from dozens of options. It taught them to assemble the furniture themselves, and to pick up the items in a store without waiting weeks for delivery. It taught them to expect great design at a low price. It taught them to bring the kids to the store and make shopping a family experience. About the only thing IKEA has not done is teach customers how to pronounce its products' names.

New Ideas vs. Changed Ideas

One of the reasons entrepreneurial firms are so successful at training new customers is that they employ the psychological phenomena known as *anchoring* and *conservatism*. Anchoring is the tendency to rely heavily on the first piece of information acquired on a subject. Conservatism is the tendency to insufficiently revise one's belief when presented with new evidence. Entrepreneurial firms quickly learn that by mixing these two tendencies, it can be easier to teach a new idea than to change an existing idea.

When a company invents something truly new, and

people actually realize that it is new, that information gets its own "storage space" in their memory.[83] This is a huge advantage for the company occupying that new mental real estate, for once individuals open up to a new idea, they are primed to learn much more about that idea. In other words, once your customers are paying attention it is much easier to teach them about the rest of your Innovation Stack. Your customers become *anchored* to your message and *conservative* toward your competition.

Conversely, anyone trying to steal your customers faces a massive challenge: either copy your Innovation Stack, which is nearly impossible, or retrain the customers, which is just supremely difficult.

Retraining is much more difficult than teaching something new. To retrain people, first you must get them to dislodge their current belief; but people have a strong tendency to think that their beliefs are immutable facts that never change.[84] So, since they are "right," they have no reason to pay attention to new information. People think they already know, so they just ignore alternative viewpoints. Then, even if you succeed in dislodging their current belief, you must still do the work of explaining something new. Unless you

---

[83] Yes, this is a massive oversimplification of how we currently believe memory functions, but the central thesis is correct.

[84] We are so certain of ourselves that psychologists have distinguished fifteen cognitive biases we use to justify our beliefs: effort justification, egocentric bias, confirmation bias, congruence bias, post-purchase rationalization, choice-supportive bias, selective perception, observer-expectancy effect, experimenter's bias, observer effect, expectation bias, ostrich effect, subjective validation, continued influence effect, and Semmelweis reflex. Wow.

really grab these individuals' attention, they will ignore all of your beautiful logic.

Which is not to say that training customers the first time is easy. There are dozens of challenges to conveying a new idea, far too many to discuss here. But I have found three major problems that are particularly damaging to entrepreneurial firms with new ideas: I call them the Curse of Knowledge, Linguistic Gravity, and Feedback Failure.

The Curse of Knowledge

Intimate familiarity has its downside. When I went to college, the bigger your stereo system, the cooler you were. My friend had a massive example, with a preamp, an amplifier, a sonic equalizer, six input sources, an isolated power supply, and several other magically glowing gadgets. The equipment consumed an entire bookshelf and eliminated the need for heating in the winter. Unfortunately, actually playing a song on this techno-tower required no fewer than seven separate operations.

One evening, my friend hosted a party for a group of people including a lady with whom he was intimately familiar and, as luck would have it, her husband. Everything was going fine until someone requested music. This lady calmly approached the wall of stereo equipment and flipped the seven switches with an unconsciously fluid competence that would make any airline captain proud. The husband, however, could not believe that his wife (who had pretended to get lost on the drive over to help hide the fact that she had a toothbrush in the medicine cabinet) was an audio system savant. Another victim of the Curse of Knowledge.

Even if your marriage depends on it, there is no way to appreciate the complexity of what you already know. Take a look into the cockpit of any airliner and you will find a dizzying array of controls. The cockpit is such a complex environment that commercial airplanes don't actually have keys: if you can fly it, you can have it. But if you watch experienced pilots fly a plane, you will notice them effortlessly flipping switches and pushing buttons without any signs of stress. They have spent enough time in this complex environment to become comfortable. Not only have they mastered a complicated system, but they have also become *unaware* of their level of mastery.

Even if we are trying to think about it, we cannot appreciate the complexity of anything with which we are intimately familiar. Intimate familiarity can be bad if you are trying to teach a customer something new or if you are trying to hide an extramarital affair. What seems as obvious as opening the bleed air switch after starting the APU[85] can confuse a new customer. As a result, many entrepreneurs fail to adequately explain how their systems work.

Linguistic Gravity

While the concept I call Linguistic Gravity is not listed in any textbook, its effects have plagued me for decades. Linguistic

---

[85] Duh.

Gravity applies to things that are somewhat similar to what people already understand. Certain words can create the wrong ideas, especially if those ideas are almost, but not quite, correct.

For instance, think about the word *farm* and notice the thoughts it creates. You may have pictured green plants, open fields, sunlight, maybe some livestock or an irrigation system. The problem of Linguistic Gravity comes when we want to farm mushrooms.

Growing mushrooms is almost antithetical to traditional farming. Mushroom farms are dark, humid caves. It would probably be better to use the word *sewer*, but that would never get past the marketing department.

The problem is that since your truly innovative new product is *sort of* close to something the customers already understand, they just stop listening. Your innovative product will be assumed to be the same as what they know, and it is very difficult to get them to even pay enough attention to learn the difference. Like black holes, the gravity of a word we know pulls all similar thoughts into it. Even if your product is truly different, people may ignore your message because of the words you choose.

Imagine you have just invented the submarine and are trying to explain it to me. Since I have never seen a submarine before, you describe it as an underwater car. Once I hear the word *car*, I picture something that moves along the bottom of the sea on four wheels and would likely get stuck among all the garbage on the ocean floor or fall into the Mariana Trench. I now have an incorrect picture in my mind and conclude that your invention is useless. Since I "know" your invention is useless, I don't listen to the rest of your explanation.

The danger of Linguistic Gravity is particularly great for entrepreneurs, as we often choose words from the industry we are expanding or improving. One of the early problems facing Southwest Airlines was simply the word *airline*, which at the time connoted an exclusive and expensive means of travel. People would hear the word *airline* and incorrectly assume that they could not afford to fly. Southwest battled this preconception by including the descriptor *low-cost* with *airline* in all its communications.

Feedback Failure

If your message is confusing or garbled, there is a good chance you will never know because of Feedback Failure, or the tendency for people to hide their contempt or confusion. In other words, people are very good at giving incorrect positive feedback. In fact, my wife and I are currently in the process of teaching our son how to provide incorrect feedback, albeit under the guise of good manners. Yes, okra is "slimy glop," but the ambassador was very nice to invite our whole family, so eat your vegetables, kid. A large part of having good manners is not saying what you truly believe.

Early in my career as a glass artist I learned that very few people would give me honest feedback about my work. I would put two pieces next to each other, ask someone's opinion, and receive vague positive responses for both pieces. The only accurate feedback I would get was when a piece sold, or more likely didn't sell, in a gallery.

Feedback Failure almost destroyed the national expansion of my nonprofit, LaunchCode Foundation, and it was totally my fault. I started LaunchCode in St. Louis as a way to solve the programmer shortage by providing job placement and free training for new programmers. When we first began the program, we had no idea if it would work because we purposely did everything differently from other institutions. LaunchCode begins by getting companies to agree to hire talented programmers who complete our certification. Once the jobs are identified, we then teach the necessary skills for free to anyone who is willing to learn. In other words, we begin with the job opening, not the education. It was completely backward compared with existing educational approaches, but it worked.

The experiment worked so well, we expanded the program to South Florida, which had an even worse talent shortage than St. Louis. But unlike the St. Louis experiment, when I landed in Miami I was armed with several dozen stories of how LaunchCode truly helped people. I had a video of an ex-Marine telling how LaunchCode got him his first job in ten years and how he was so proud to support his family without government help.

But telling those stories almost killed our Florida efforts. Every employer I spoke with said they were eager to participate, and then they would not do anything. They loved (or said they loved) what we were doing, and then would not hire our graduates. They needed the talent; we had the talent. What was wrong?

It was only after a year of failing to place programmers into jobs that I found out what the Feedback Failure was. One day I was trying to reach the CIO of Florida's largest health-care conglomerate, but instead was given a meeting with the "Diversity Officer." So because LaunchCode was actually helping people get programming jobs, and some of these people looked different from the stereotypical computer programmer, the employers thought our people were not talented!

The companies were thinking, "We don't want to hire people who need jobs, we want to hire people with talent." The Linguistic Gravity of LaunchCode being a nonprofit charitable organization, combined with my stories of helping people, was enough to translate, in their minds, into "I'll hire LaunchCode's people when I need to improve my diversity numbers, but right now I need talent." Of course, nobody would ever say such a thing, they were far too "polite," so I also had Feedback Failure. Once we stopped talking about helping people, companies started hiring our graduates.[86]

Moments of Wow

Teaching anything requires the attention of the student. But how many things do we really pay attention to? If neuroscientists are to be believed, we ignore most of what we

---

[86] We all do this. Imagine you need heart surgery and the hospital says, "We have a guy who really deserved a chance to be a doctor."

actually perceive, so how can you get someone to pay attention to your new product or new idea? Ideally, you would
delight your customers with an experience that is so extraordinary that they notice. This was the reason that I kept
the Square reader so small that it was slightly difficult to
use. The small size was important in getting people's attention since they had never seen something that small read a
credit card. But another thing was also happening, something that might make you uncomfortable if you learned
what it was. Actually, making you slightly uncomfortable
was my goal.

Our reader was, and still is, so small that it requires a bit
of practice before people learn to swipe correctly. It is small
enough to grab your attention, and then it is slightly difficult to
use, so you pay even more attention. But at the same time you
are paying attention to our reader, you are learning the name
of our company and probably talking with your own customer
about how much it costs and how easy it is to sign up.

This is formally known as the *processing difficulty effect*:[87]
people tend to remember things better if they go through a
struggle to learn them. I had unintentionally stumbled on a
way to get even more attention on our products. We taught
millions of people to teach millions of other people about
Square.

Do you remember how uncomfortable it felt to take your
first ride share? I clearly remember standing on a sidewalk as

---

[87] E. J. O'Brien and J. L. Myers (1985). "When comprehension difficulty im-
proves memory for text." *Journal of Experimental Psychology: Learning,
Memory, and Cognition* 11(1): 12–21.

a gleaming black Dodge Charger pulled up. When it came to being a passenger in a car, at that time I had only two models in my mind. One was the taxi ride, where I sat in the back and tried not to touch anything or let the driver see me memorizing his license number. My other model was riding with a friend, in which case I would sit in the front seat and talk the whole trip. Then this black Charger pulled up and I had to pick the front door or the back door. Well, it was clearly not a taxi, so climbing in the back felt rude; but I didn't know the driver, so riding up front seemed presumptuous. I rode up front and felt totally uncomfortable, and probably so did the driver. Uber and Lyft were new and I hadn't yet been trained.

But that moment of discomfort was important, for it got my attention. I thought about how convenient it was to hail a ride from my phone, how I liked the fact that the driver and I both earned ratings, and how I loved getting out of the car without fumbling for cash after the cabbie said the credit card machine was broken. Uber had just trained me. Later it trained me to sit in the back. Eventually, it trained me to ride with Lyft. I now have three models in my brain for being a passenger: taxi, friend, and ride share. Discomfort in my first ride share was good, because Uber had to teach me a new way to travel, and I learned it.

The IKEA Effect

IKEA has so perfected grabbing the customer's attention that it now has its own formally recognized cognitive bias. Clipboard-toting psychologists actually refer to a phenomenon known as the *IKEA effect.*[88] Simply put, the frustrating act of assembling your own furniture causes you to fall in love with the final product.

That 6mm Allen wrench in your hands is not just connecting two pieces of laminated sawdust, it is also rewiring your brain. Even if the completed piece of furniture is missing parts and needs to be braced against the wall to not kill the cat, you will value it more highly because of the time you spent creating it.

IKEA, in fact, has a long history of making its customers just uncomfortable enough to learn the IKEA way. From the original line around the building for a showroom that was not part of the furniture fair, to the modern store where you deposit your kids into a ball pit, IKEA demands your attention.

Southwest also knew how to get your attention, especially in the early days. If you didn't notice the flight attendant uniforms, which made miniskirts look like muumuus, it had a dozen other slightly jarring experiences. My favorite was lounge seating: two rows of seats that faced each other. The lounge configuration was fantastic if you had five friends along for the ride, and terrible if you had to stare into some stranger's lap for the whole flight. But it sure was different!

A. P. Giannini also wanted the experience in his bank to be memorable. In many ways this was guaranteed, since many Bank of Italy customers had never been to a bank, so the whole experience was new. To make sure the lessons could be

---

[88] M. I. Norton, D. Mochon, and D. Ariely. "The 'IKEA effect': When labor leads to love." *Journal of Consumer Psychology* 22(3): 453–60.

learned, Giannini insisted that his tellers speak their clients' native languages. Managers were hired for their gregarious disposition in addition to their financial acumen.[89]

It doesn't matter how innovative your product is if the customers ignore it. Getting someone's attention can make all the difference, but the entrepreneurial company has some natural advantages in this battle against the Curse of Knowledge, Linguistic Gravity, and Feedback Failure.

WHEN JACK AND I started Square, all we knew was that one small merchant in St. Louis had a problem. We could not tell if anyone besides me would ever use the product: it was so new that there was no way to test that. Eventually, we won the attention of millions of people who found value in what we were building. We trained those people in an entirely new way, and they in turn are now training us. Our unique products, in the hands of millions of customers, generate billions of unique interactions. As a result of these billions of customer interactions, Square's invisible army is now a critical part of our Innovation Stack.

Our customers buy, sell, develop, and defend our products. We are in business for and because of this invisible army. They keep us company. And we show our respect for these customers in a way that I wish more companies would copy.

---

[89] Gerald Nash. *A. P. Giannini and the Bank of America* (Norman: University of Oklahoma Press, 1992).

CHAPTER 15

Low, Not Lowest

PRICING is a deceptively complex subject. On one hand, nothing is simpler to understand than a price. It's a single number, and usually one that is under control of the company creating the product or service. Is the way entrepreneurial companies set their prices any different from how normal businesses do it? It is, and this difference is both subtle and profound.

Low vs. Lowest

Is there any difference between having a *low* price and the *lowest* price? The English language barely distinguishes between these two phrases, but the difference is important. In many cases, an entrepreneurial company's low price is also the lowest price in the market. The actual price is less important than the way this price was derived. If we look past the price tag and focus on the logic behind the number, a subtle but important difference appears between entrepreneurial firms and most other companies.

While studying entrepreneurs across the ages, I found a recurring emphasis on *low* prices, as opposed to having the *lowest* price. *Low* price results from a company philosophy to constantly deliver maximum value to the customer. Entrepreneurs strive to keep price as low as possible, while still maintaining the quality of the overall experience. The *lowest* price, in contrast, requires a comparison with another company selling a similar product or service. A company that values having the lowest price must constantly look over its shoulder to see what the competition is doing.

Southwest Airlines had prices so low that it was stealing traffic from the bus lines. Herb told me, "In the 1990s an independent study concluded that Southwest provided 90 percent of all the low-fare competition in America." It was not unusual in the early days to see a $69 fare on Southwest while the major airlines were charging $400 for the same routing. But during this time, Southwest was also focused on the quality of the customer experience. Herb explained, "From when they started keeping statistics at the Department of Transportation, we had the number one on-time record, the number one baggage-handling record, and the number one record with respect to customer complaints. So obviously people were getting something they liked because our complaint ratio was way below the other carriers for decades."

But Herb was quick to emphasize that having a low price never relieved Southwest of its need to deliver the best customer experience. "A big failure of a number of companies is they get into an *either-or* mode. You know, 'We can have low prices *or* good customer service but we can't have both,'" Herb told me.

It's Kamprad's ironing board dilemma: you can't make everything so cheap that the quality suffers. IKEA's lesson from the ironing board battle with Gunnars was to not focus on having the lowest price in the market, but instead having a low price on a high-quality product. IKEA soon learned to sell at a low price and ignore what competitors were doing. To this day, IKEA will still reduce the price of an item even when it has no competition.

An audacious entrepreneur sets a low price even when the competition is far more expensive. In its early days, the Bank of Italy kept interest rates at 7 percent, almost a third less than other banks. And during this time the Bank of Italy was also the most accommodating bank for its customers in a dozen other ways.

When Jack and I set the initial pricing for Square's service, typical rates for credit card processing exceeded 4 percent for small businesses. We set a price of 2.75 percent despite the fact that 3 percent or more would have been possible. We also eliminated all other fees, including the per transaction fee that every other institution charged. We have continued to lower our rates and increase our services as conditions allow.

Low Price vs. Competition

Having a low price can paradoxically mean *not* lowering it in the face of competition. When Amazon undercut our 2.75 percent rate with a rate of 1.95 percent, we did not respond. Our price was set as low as we could manage while still maintaining our business. If we could have been charging less, we would have been. The attacks of even the world's most feared competitor did not change that calculus. Imagine what would have happened if we had matched Amazon's price only to raise it back up once Amazon abandoned the market: our customers would never trust Square again.

Entrepreneurial companies are focused not on their competitors, but on their customers. Even when they do respond to a competitor, they do it with a focus on their own customers, as Southwest did during its $13 fare war.

Building an Innovation Stack will give your firm the ability to set prices differently from other companies. If you want to change your price, that change should originate from the Innovation Stack. Low price is a result.

Why Low?

Is low price altruistic? Does an entrepreneur have to be motivated to square up or help "the little fellow"? It's hard to say, especially since all the entrepreneurs I studied became billionaires many times over. It's easy to be altruistic if you are one of the richest people on the planet. Giannini himself would have been the richest man in the world had he not constantly given away his personal wealth throughout his life. So let's assume, just for the sake of investigation, that entrepreneurs are not universally altruistic. We know this from Kamprad's politics. Does low price still make sense? It does in three important ways: customer trust, corporate alignment, and competitive advantage.

Low Price and Customer Trust

Trust is a precious and delicate thing. To illustrate how difficult it is to evaluate trust, join me on a quick thought experiment. Think for a minute how many people you would trust to take all your money, keep it safe for a year, and then return it to you.

Now ask yourself, what is the difference between someone you trust and someone you don't? The difference is subtle. In fact, if you were forced to justify your preferences you would probably be unable to do so in a way that would pass muster in court, or even in conversation. But you know. OK, now think about something else before you lose all your friends.

My point is simply that trust is elusive and subtle even in the case of people we know. It is even more difficult for a company to earn our trust. Strategies for building customer trust can backfire, and those who seek our trust may be least deserving of it. But among the limited tools we do have for building trust, pricing is perhaps the most powerful.

Low price forges a stronger relationship with customers by building trust in the brand. I remember the first time I had to get across the country fast—it was an emergency—and I discovered Southwest Airlines. The fare was a tenth of what I would have been willing to pay under those circumstances, and that got my attention. The second time I went to fly, I was curious. After a dozen more such experiences, I was hooked.

Conversely, when a customer has no choice, companies *can* extract massive premiums. The customer may pay, but will also remember.

Customer trust is even more important for an entrepreneurial company that depends on training its invisible army to behave differently, as we saw in the previous chapter. A *consistently* low price creates trust. This trust can be strong enough for a customer to use a separate airline reservation system, travel hours to buy furniture, or place his or her savings in an upstart bank. When we launch a new product at Square, our customers' trust gives us a precious moment of attention to introduce a new idea.

Trust, however, can be destroyed by one event. Burn a customer once and that person will avoid doing business with you unless there is no other option. This is why low price must be consistent in order to gain and retain customer trust. Customers may not trust you until the fifth or fiftieth time you deliver on the low price promise. But eventually they do, and then the magic happens.

Customers who trust you are more valuable than customers who love you. Love can be won and lost, but you only get one shot at trust. It is a rarer emotion. Customers who trust your company become your best salespeople. They buy your products without the usual comparison shopping. They eagerly await your latest thing. Sometimes they wait outside your stores for you to open. And they actually feel happy about all of this because they love your firm. Love is a side effect of trust.

Low Price and Corporate Alignment

Beyond the trust of customers, low price creates corporate alignment: the ability to have everyone on your team sharing the same values. When your coworkers see evidence that the company is not exploiting every pricing advantage, they see that the company values its customers. After all, a company that will exploit its customers will usually exploit its workers first. Employees can become even more cynical than customers because they interact with the company daily, and thus they are more likely to see (or even cause) abuses. A cynical employee who meets a skeptical customer creates a downward spiral of negativity.

Price is part of culture. Every firm I studied used low price not only as a metric to measure, but also as a way to demonstrate how they valued their customers, a value everyone could see reflected on the price tag.

Running a world-changing company requires thousands of employees to make millions of decisions. Herb estimated that Southwest employees have over two hundred million annual interactions with customers. Each encounter depends on the employee making a good decision, and Southwest literally burned the rule book back in the 1980s to empower employees to make good decisions based on their alignment with the corporate culture instead of some forced obligation.

So how do you control thousands of employees? You basically don't. There are not enough cameras or corporate email bots or thousand-page loose-leaf folders to get people to behave if they don't first believe. Beyond about a dozen people, control succumbs to culture. And price has a huge impact on culture because it is so visible.

Imagine a company that has just invented a way to lower the cost of producing its product. It has two choices: keep the savings or share it with the customers. It may seem like the better choice from the company's perspective is to keep the money. But keeping all the money sends two dangerous messages to the employees. The first is: *watch out, you work for a place that will take everything it can get.* The other message is: *we value short-term gains over long-term goodwill.* You might want to keep your résumé updated at that firm.

When Southwest lowers a price on a route with no competition, or Square adds another free feature, or IKEA drops the price of a chair, these actions are witnessed by thousands of employees and millions of customers.

Low Price and Competitive Advantage

Low price protects the entrepreneurial company from competition. Keeping prices low even when there is no immediate competition leaves little room for new entrants. By dropping prices to a low point in all markets, the entrepreneur ensures that these copycats have no room for error.

Let's say that your Innovation Stack allows you to sell your product for $5 when the nearest competition is selling something similar for $10. If your competition wants to match your price, that company will need to copy most if not all of the elements of your Innovation Stack or create a Stack of its own. We saw in chapter 12 that this was nearly mathematically impossible. Making a jump from $10 down to $5 is too big a chasm to cross in one jump. Most of your competitors will just quit.

But now consider the same situation where you are charging $9, still the *lowest* price, but not a *low* price. In this case, a competitor may be able to copy one or two elements of your Stack and sell for $8. Of course, you can now drop your price to $7, but your competitor still needs to implement only one or two more elements from your Stack to drop its price to $6. Of course, you can still go down to $5. But now you have competition only a dollar away and it may be able to catch you.

By "maximizing profit" at every step, you give your competitors breathing room as they slowly copy your Innovation Stack. As we saw in chapter 13, the math of copying a few elements is relatively easy. If you adjust your price in response to competitors who are slowly replicating your innovation, you create an easier environment for them. Conversely, if you reflect every efficiency of your Innovation

Stack in your low price, your competitors will be forced to attempt everything at once and will likely quit or fail.

But Wait, There's More

Innovation Stacks that include low price also create a self-reinforcing positive loop. All your customers who refuse to go to your competitors are precious resources. All their feedback goes to you and keeps your Innovation Stack growing. Low price and the trust it builds are two of the main reasons that these customers stick with you. Having a market to yourself is about much more than a captive group of customers who will not or cannot buy elsewhere. The interactions with all those customers is a source of inspiration and innovation and can help you maintain your lead for decades.

Some Bad Examples

The best way to evaluate how low price creates, or perhaps preserves, competitive advantage is to see what happens when a company abandons it. Unfortunately for them but good for answering this question, two of the firms I have studied in this book have now abandoned low price.

Bank of Italy, which became Bank of America, had a massive advantage over the other banks during Giannini's lifetime. After Giannini, the bank began to disregard its customers, especially when it came to price. As I write this, Bank of America is the second-most-hated company in

America.[90] Its specialty is charging small customers ridiculous fees[91] for overdrafts and other minor transgressions.

Southwest gave up low price about the same time Herb retired in 2008. For the next five years, while other carriers increased their prices an average of 8 percent annually, Southwest's prices climbed over 30 percent. After this increase Southwest's prices were 17 percent to 145 percent *higher* than its competitors.[92] In 2018, Southwest, along with American, Delta, and United, settled a price-fixing lawsuit by the US Department of Justice.

Did Southwest's changing its pricing change its competitive position in the industry? Let's look at the results. Twenty-two[93] low-cost airlines tried to compete with Southwest during Herb's tenure, and every one failed except JetBlue. (JetBlue also embraced low price, won special landing rights in the nation's busiest city,[94] and had its own Innovation Stack.) Low price protected Southwest Airlines for four decades.

But since Southwest abandoned low price in 2008, five new airlines now compete with Southwest and *are all succeeding*

---

[90] Samuel Stebbins et al., "America's Most Hated Companies," 24/7 Wall St., January 22, 2018.

[91] Ryan Grenoble, "Bank of America's Poorest Customers to Be Charged for Checking," *Huffington Post*, January 24, 2018.

[92] Bill McGee, "RIP to the 'Southwest Effect'"? *USA Today*, May 19, 2014.

[93] Air Florida, AirTran, ATA, Hooters Air, Independence Air, Metrojet, Midway, National, Pacific Southwest, Pearl Air, People Express, Safe Air, Skybus, SkyValue, Song, Southeast, Streamline Air, Ted, Tower Air, ValuJet, Vanguard, and Western Pacific Airlines.

[94] JetBlue got seventy-five landing slots at JFK the year it launched, giving it a huge market advantage.

over a decade later.[95] I'm sure there are many things that have changed since Herb retired, but the only one I've noticed as a customer is that Southwest no longer gives me a reliably low price. I remember the first time I found American Airlines had a lower price than Southwest. At first I thought that this price was just another bug in American's notoriously unstable reservations system,[96] but soon the pattern was clear. Twenty years of my trusting Southwest, gone like the space in the overhead bin.

Southwest is still a great company with a lot of its original Innovation Stack intact. It now also has massive economies of scale, and it is still doing well. But I wonder how many of those other carriers would be flying if Southwest was still *the* low price airline. I really wanted to ask Herb about this, but I never had the guts during our first visit. It seemed disrespectful to a man who was super generous with his time. Tragically, Herb died before I could correct my mistake. I apologize both to the reader and to Herb.

IKEA, despite the recent death of its founder, seems nowhere near abandoning its low price philosophy. It is, perhaps as a result, dominating the furniture market across the planet. Even in hypercompetitive China, no store can even get close to replicating IKEA's price and quality.

When an entrepreneurial firm abandons low price as a philosophy, it makes more money for a while. These massive

---

[95] Allegiant, Frontier, JetBlue, and Spirit Airlines. Virgin America was also successful and then acquired by Alaska Airlines.

[96] Sabre, the Semi-Automated Business Research Environment. Oh, what a beautiful mess.

profits, however, may attract the attention of a new competitor, and if there is enough money in the market to sustain that new competitor, then the first company no longer has the market or customers to itself. If a new competitor has room to undercut the firm's prices, then it's a double whammy because it also quickly loses customer trust.

How Low Do You Go?

In a market where everyone copies everyone else, there isn't much leeway to lower price. Even if you gain a temporary advantage, your competitors will soon copy you and catch up, so you might want to take the fleeting windfall and plop it in the bank.[97]

But having an Innovation Stack affords entrepreneurial companies the flexibility to have a lower price. An Innovation Stack creates wide margin between the costs of production and the value of the product in the customer's mind. Economists call this margin *excess value*, and it represents the maximum amount that a customer is theoretically willing to pay. Prices can be easily adjusted to capture this "excess value." If your customers will pay more, why not charge more?

In fact, one of the first things you learn at business school is how to efficiently make such price adjustments. While such behavior may make sense to a regular company,

---

[97] Well, if that bank is the Bank of America, make sure you meet the minimum balance requirement, or you'll be sorry.

it's a mistake for the entrepreneur. Then again, none of the entrepreneurs I studied attended business school, and they all chose to keep their price low. I'll let Herb have the last word here.

"We never tried to maximize revenue the way other companies do. I was interviewed for some guru's magazine and this guy asks, 'How do you maximize your revenues?' and I said, 'We don't.' And he said, 'You don't strive to maximize your revenues?' I said, 'Absolutely not. We have the lowest costs in the industry by far. If we try to maximize revenues we would be giving away our strongest, sharpest competitive weapon, which is the fact that our low costs enable us to charge low fares.'"

Herb was particularly keen to explain to me that Southwest's pricing was based on having a low price and *not reacting to the competition.* "We really thought that if we charge different fares all over our system, depending on the amount of competition we have, then we are reacting to them, and busting up our brand as *the* low-fare airline."

CHAPTER 16

Disrupting Disruption

A T the outset of this book, I
made the claim that copying was the strongest force in the
world. We are so predisposed to copy that it infiltrates our
most innovative institutions, even within that self-proclaimed
hub of innovative thinking, Silicon Valley. Of course, we
don't call ourselves *copycats* in the Valley, we call ourselves
disrupters.

How could I make the accusation that people committed to disruption, to the very destruction of a system, are
really copying? It is a matter of focus. If your goal is to disrupt something, you must at least know what you are dis-
rupting. But simply looking at the industry you want to
disrupt will cause you to emulate it in countless ways. Ironically, to focus on disruption is to invite copying to dominate your thoughts. The ball goes where you look.

At Square we resisted hiring anyone from the payments
industry for years. Actually, during our first week in business I found a payments expert who offered to consult with

us, but we terminated that relationship almost immediately. His advice was straight from the industry we were trying to avoid copying, and it seemed foolish to pay someone to explain how to do everything we didn't want to do. For the next several years, we avoided getting anyone with payment DNA into our company. This allowed us to think freely about what new things we wanted to build and not about how it had always been done.

Three years ago when I began writing this book I immediately stopped reading all nonfiction.[98] I was simply afraid that I would read some great book and it would force my thoughts to copy what had already been done, even if this reaction was unconscious. My intellectual quarantine was the price I had to pay for the chance to actually express an original thought.

Another Dying Word

Disruption has become nearly as threadbare a concept as entrepreneurship. The two words could be roommates at rehab. When Clayton Christensen first popularized the disruption concept back in 1997, the idea was novel and interesting. But what Christensen originally called *disruptive innovation* has now been shortened to just *disruption* and the oversimplification is profound.

Two decades later, disruption has become the high-fructose corn syrup of business, an overused ingredient sprayed on

---

[98] My single exception was to read John Doerr's great book on OKRs, *Measure What Matters*, because we use OKRs to manage my new company.

pitches and injected into keynotes in the hope of disguising the familiar taste of conformity. Silicon Valley now has an annual conference called simply "Disrupt." I hear pitches every month from start-ups wishing to destroy the economics of some existing industry. Hidden—frequently well hidden—inside these pitches is the implication that the invisible hand of the economy will reallocate resources so that we will all be better off and enjoy a more efficient world after the carnage. It doesn't always happen that way.

Craigslist certainly disrupted classified advertising, one of the main revenue sources for newspapers. The papers responded by reducing their news-gathering operations—firing reporters who collectively watched all our backs. How many more scandals would have been exposed if those now-unemployed reporters were still on the beat?[99] We can never know. Disruption is not always positive.

But a more dangerous aspect of disruption is its retrograde focus. Just as having the lowest price means focusing on competitors instead of customers, venerating disruption means focusing on old systems that somehow need to be dismantled or destroyed. Indeed, some existing systems deserve the wrecking ball, but to make destruction of the incumbents the focus of entrepreneurship distracts attention from the creative potential of innovation. There is another path.

As I studied the great entrepreneurs of history I expected to find a large swath of disruption and destruction. I

---

[99] This is my newest perfect problem. Check out invisibly.com. And I have no idea if it will work.

found instead something far more positive. The vast majority of entrepreneurial ventures did not steal their customers from any established business, but rather brought new people into a market. Optimism, innovation, and inclusion are the buzzwords of those who expand markets. Disruption deserves to be disrupted.

Dis-what?

Jack and I began with the initial goal of building a new base under the pyramid of credit card acceptance. As I type these words, Square merchants represent a healthy fraction of all US businesses accepting credit cards. And yes, we count that lemonade stand and my friend Bob. But to existing merchants and their credit card providers, Square caused remarkably little, if any, disruption. In ten years, Square and its customers have created that new base under the pyramid, and we get credited in Silicon Valley for being a disruptive company. So what did we disrupt?

When we entered the market in 2009, Heartland Payment Systems was teetering on the edge of bankruptcy, having barely survived the largest data breach in history. A decade later Heartland is still in business, along with every other major credit card–processing firm that existed when we started. True, some of these firms merged or were bought out, but that cycle has been happening in the credit card industry since its beginning. In some ways we compete directly with PayPal, but PayPal is now an order of magnitude larger than it was when we started. So, what did we disrupt again?

How Big Is the Market?

How long is the British coastline? The answer to this famous question, of course, is that it depends on how you measure it.[100] Markets are infinite. If they appear finite, it is likely because we are incorporating the biases of the existing market. Within the confines of an established market the walls look solid and the market finite. Such thinking looks ridiculous in hindsight, but may appear real at the time. Add innovation and entrepreneurship and the wall becomes a horizon.

When Southwest was beginning, the prevailing "wisdom" was that only the rich wanted to fly places. Of course, at the time, only the rich *could* fly places, but that doesn't mean that regular people *wanted* to stay on the ground. The bigger question for T-shirt–clad disrupters is this: did Southwest's success in welcoming new people into the skies disrupt the other carriers?

With the possible exception of the former communist bloc, no market has seen as much disruption as the airlines. There have been roughly two hundred airline bankruptcies in the United States since Southwest began, but did

---

[100] B. Mandelbrot (1967). "How long is the coast of Britain? Statistical self-similarity and fractional dimension." *Science* 156(3775): 636–38.

Southwest cause this disruption? Interestingly, it may be the opposite. The success of Southwest may have saved some of the other airlines.

In my visit with Herb Kelleher, he proudly noted that Southwest didn't drive other airlines out of business, but rather increased the total number of travelers. "When we went into the Dallas–Houston market in '71 it was the thirty-fourth-largest market in the United States. We were there one year and it grew to be the fifth largest. So in other words, we were just taking all of these people that had never flown and putting them on airplanes for the first time. But the remarkable thing is that *all the other carriers increased their traffic on that route as well.* We weren't taking business from anyone, we were growing the market." And the effect was not just in the Dallas–Houston market. Herb told me, "We come into new cities, and traffic increases by 272 percent in the first year."

But if Southwest was so good for air travel, why did TWA, Pan Am, Braniff, United, Continental, Northwest, US Airways, and two hundred other US carriers plummet into bankruptcy? The best explanation is not Southwest, but deregulation. When the government deregulated air travel in 1978, the highfliers stopped faster than a tailgating motorcyclist.

In other words, it was not Southwest's entry into the market that destroyed the other airlines, it was the chaos of removing forty years' worth of government protection from the market. This explains why international carriers like Pan Am that never directly competed with Southwest were permanently grounded.

Did IKEA disrupt the furniture market? Again the data says otherwise. Fortunately, in 2015 IKEA opened its first store in South Korea, which provides an excellent test case. When IKEA opened its first store there, the two local South Korean furniture makers Hanssem and Iloom both saw increases in their sales, some as high as 10 percent. In fact, the entire South Korean furniture market, which had been flat for two decades, saw an unprecedented 7 percent growth the year IKEA arrived.[101]

Was there disruption? Certainly a lot of Korean furniture companies have disappeared; nearly half ceased operations between 2011 and 2016. But this downfall began four years before IKEA entered the market, so it's hard to attribute all change to the Swedish giant.

If any of the companies I investigated disrupted a market that was already in place, it would be Bank of Italy. What we think of today as banking was largely invented by A. P. Giannini and his team. Their model so dominated the world of banking that eventually all the other banks copied it. This transformation took decades, and it is fair to assert that the old banking model of serving only a select elite indeed has mostly ended. But the individual banks themselves are still there. The Bank of New York, Chase, Citibank, Citizens, Fifth Third, Goldman Sachs, Hancock, Lazard, M&T, Mellon, Northern Trust, Oppenheimer, PNC, Regions, and Wells Fargo have all existed for over a century.

---

[101] "Two Years On, Ikea Korea Impact Gauged," December 16, 2016, Inside-Retail.asia.

IS DISRUPTION BAD? Not by itself. But disruption has also never been the focus of good entrepreneurs. The entrepreneurs profiled in this book set out to build and not to destroy. To focus on disruption is to look over one's shoulder into the past. But if you are trying to solve a perfect problem or expand a market, shouldn't you study that industry? No, you look at your customers, or I should say your potential customers, for they do not even know your product or service is possible.

William Gibson famously observed, "The future is already here—it's just not evenly distributed." Unfair as this situation sounds, Gibson's words contain a hopeful promise: while only a few of us enjoy the latest cool thing, eventually the future will deliver it to us all. But who will make that delivery?

Entrepreneurs distribute that future. The companies they build are not disrupters, they are market expanders for those people waiting for their slice of the future.

If disruption occurs, it is merely a side effect. The focus of the entrepreneur is the people who cannot get a loan, or travel, or furnish their home, or get paid. The focus of the entrepreneur is on the horizon beyond the wall. If we glance at the system, it is neither to copy it nor to destroy it, but simply to see how much more can be done.

CHAPTER 17

How It Feels

WE spend our lives mostly limited to solutions that have been created by others. We often consider unsolved problems to be unsolvable, but this is wrong. The purpose of this book is to show you that you don't have to limit yourself to what has been done before. Becoming an entrepreneur is possible, but it will feel strange. So, in this chapter I want to prepare you mentally for some of that discomfort by discussing how it feels to me.

Feelings are deeply personal, so studying them is difficult. Luckily, I got to meet Herb Kelleher, who inspired much of this book. But entrepreneurs like Herb are rare, so my other guides I have only met through the pages of history. These histories consist largely of impressive business statistics and the occasional amusing story. I would love to have had just one hour with A. P. Giannini—or Sam Walton or Andrew Carnegie. I would not have asked them how they did it. I would ask them *how it felt*.

Feelings are understandably absent from the historical record, which makes perfect sense. Emotions are something we Americans usually don't discuss, and most interviews are conducted only after an entrepreneur has become wildly successful. It's pretty hard to imagine some reporter saying, "So, now that you are one of the most powerful people on the planet, tell me about your inner child."

But this is what I always wanted to know! How did it feel? Were they scared? Why didn't they quit? I wanted to ask my mentor, but he had inconveniently died before I was born. I asked anyway.

Humility

The reason you may never have heard about A. P. Giannini is not because of the way he lived and the things he did; it is because of the way he died, and the things he didn't do. Here was a man who entered a burning, lawless city and emerged with two cartloads of gold. Giannini swam a river to make a sale. He looked, led, and lived like a superhero. He also had a knack for dramatic language, once noting, "No man actually owns a fortune, it owns him." In fact, most of A. P. Giannini's quotations deserve to be carved in granite. But there is one thing you will not find on all that granite: his name. Giannini was profoundly humble.

A. P. Giannini never endowed any massive foundation; nor did he pass a tremendous fortune to his heirs. He built the world's largest bank from scratch without even putting his name on the door.[102] When A.P. retired in 1945, he gave half his fortune to medical research and the rest to scholarships for Bank of America employees. A.P. asked, "Why should a man pile a lot of money for somebody to spend after he's gone?" He died in 1949 with a small estate of only $439,278, a pittance compared to his peers. Modest to the end.

Giannini could have amassed the world's greatest fortune, but he chose to never even become a millionaire. He could have separated himself from everyday people, but he did precisely the opposite. He could have bragged about his success, but he deflected the attention. Seeing this behavior made me think of a word that, in contrast to *entrepreneur*, has suffered from underuse: *humility*.

Humility is an odd bird that hides in plain sight. You never hear some red-faced pundit screaming, *"I am the humblest!"* Humility is elusive, but when I looked it was right there. It was Giannini saying, "We consider the wage earner or small business man who deposits his savings regularly, no matter how small the amount may be, to be the most valuable client our bank can have." It was Kamprad in the home of a poor Italian worker asking why only the rich had beautiful things. It was Kelleher telling me how pleased he was that kids could visit their grandparents because of Southwest's low fares. It was these great entrepreneurs connecting with their fellow human beings.

---

[102] Bank of Italy offices were famous for having the managers sit out with the customers.

Humility and audacity are allies. Admitting that one does not know something frees the mind from the constraints of the known world. To actually do something new requires us to first summon the humility to admit that our solution may not work, followed by the audacity to try anyway. Hubris and overconfidence confine us to the world of already-solved problems. Nobody is "officially" qualified to be an entrepreneur.

Humility allows us to take that first step into the unknown.

Fear

Much as we praise independence, we humans are herd animals. Our peripheral vision is constantly checking to be sure that we are not acting too differently from those around us. As a species, we feel safe when we behave like others. Not surprisingly, if we behave too differently, we feel fear. Or at least I do.

People talk about being bold in the face of danger. Maybe they are telling the truth, or maybe they alter the story to sound cool. Whatever the answer, I've never learned a way to not be afraid. I have, however, learned to work effectively even when I'm scared. In fact, there are some tasks I probably could not do *without* sweaty hands.

If this were merely a business book, we could talk about boldly copying your competitors while the herd lumbers slowly along. But this is a book on entrepreneurship, and if you ever attempt some of the activities described, your company won't have any company. If you innovate, you are going to lose the comfort of the herd, and that causes fear. Better learn to deal with it.

I won't tell you not to be afraid; like I said, I've never learned how to do that. But I have learned how to perform even though I am afraid, and that seems to be sufficient. Believe it or not, fear, if properly managed, can be a huge advantage. You may as well make the monster under your bed do some cleaning while it's down there.

Fear and Learning

The last time I was blindfolded and tossed into the back of a car wasn't too scary. My brother had tied the blindfold and my father was driving. Several friends and relatives were packed in with me. The terror started when the blindfold was removed. I was standing on a runway with a small plane and a flight instructor ready to take off. "Get in, you're flying."

I've always been afraid of planes, small planes in particular; but with my entire family watching, I couldn't refuse.[103] We took off. I flew the next half hour certain that the engine would fail, causing the instructor to have a sudden brain aneurysm. After we landed, I learned that my family had all chipped in to pay for my pilot training. So I learned to fly a plane, basically terrified the entire time.

The good thing about learning a skill in a state of fear is that the lessons really take. I have now been a pilot for fifteen

---

[103] My grandfather and uncle were both pilots, in the days before GPS and weather radar.

years, and I don't think there has ever been a time in the cockpit when I have not been somewhat afraid. Twice that fear was justified. In both cases, I had to very rapidly perform a series of tasks, and in both cases I was literally in fear for my life. But here's the good news: if you learn how to perform a skill when you are afraid, it's very easy to repeat that performance when you are afraid. I'm totally familiar with handling a plane under duress; I've never flown under any other conditions.

There are basically two ways to behave when you are afraid: you can freeze or you can act. Don't freeze. Freezing in the cockpit is certain death; so one of the main things they teach in pilot school is to keep flying the plane.[104] But as long as you don't freeze, fear becomes your friend. Fear is a great motivator.

We hear the advice to "step outside our comfort zones" so often that the phrase is almost meaningless. "Comfort zone" is one of those creepy phrases that sounds like it belongs in a "Good Touch, Bad Touch" conversation, so let's just say: *get comfortable with discomfort.* Get used to what fear and discomfort are like. Think of it this way: if you're about to do something that has never been done, there is no way to rehearse the act itself. But you're probably going to be nervous when you do it, so at least practice that part.

Your conditions for practice needn't be life threatening. I practice by talking to strangers; half the population is

---

[104] The other big lesson is to ignore your body. Pilots in the clouds experience all sorts of odd and incorrect feelings. You may feel like you are diving, when you are actually climbing and about to stall. Pilots spend hundreds of hours learning to ignore their bodies and trust their training.

uncomfortable with that. And I can adjust the intensity by increasing the number of strangers. So now I do a lot of public speaking. I was once so scared in front of an audience that I literally froze on stage. I could not say a single word and somehow my salivary glands migrated to my palms: hands wet, mouth dry. Someone from the audience had to come up and help me off stage. I've now done so much public speaking that it's actually fun, but my hands still sweat.[105]

What does all this have to do with being an entrepreneur? Fear is part of innovation. It's a natural and appropriate response to being unable to verify that you are in a safe place. And while it is impossible to prepare for the feedback you will receive when you truly innovate, you can at least prepare for the way you will feel.

Feedback

Not only do entrepreneurs have fear as a companion, sometimes fear is their only companion.[106] Feedback, especially positive feedback, lags far behind innovation. In other words, if you are doing something truly innovative, you will almost certainly not have any proof when you could really use it. If you are used to a stream of frequent, mostly positive feedback, then innovation is going to feel like walk-

---

[105] Working with hot glass is similar: you get one moment to make a move and you never get that moment back. As that moment approaches, I get nervous. I get nervous when I speak. I get nervous when I fly. I get nervous when my wife says, "We need to talk." Hell, I get nervous when I have five voice mails.
[106] I have no hard data to support this, just thirty years of candid conversations with people doing amazing things.

ing into an anechoic chamber. The eerie lack of any reverberation can drive some people crazy.

It's easy to forget just how lost you felt at the beginning, especially if you ultimately manage to find your way. Think about the decision tree below: when you're at point **b** and looking back, the path you took seems clear. But when you're at point **a** and don't know the path, every forecast is a wild guess.

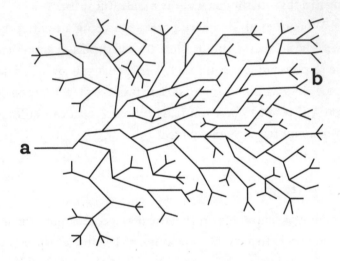

It is cruelly ironic that all the praise and admiration that we heap onto successful entrepreneurs arrives only after they have become successful. It's like receiving a Kevlar vest as a get-well present after you've been shot.

A Mass of Innovation

Perhaps the greatest mental challenge is that you have no idea how long the journey will last, or if you will ever complete it. I wish I had some great insight here, but the best I can say is that every time I have begun to build something truly new I feel just as nervous as all the previous times. Past success simply amplifies the voice in my head saying, *"Quit while you're ahead before people realize it was just luck."*

I have used the word *innovation* more than two hundred times in this book and always as a mass noun, like the word *cement.* You would never say, "We need another cement or our building will collapse." My hope is to condition you to see the interconnectedness of innovation: how one invention originates from a predecessor and necessitates a successor. If you train yourself to notice how elements of the Stack connect, you will see what others miss. You will see how changing the way passengers board a plane impacts the pilots, tickets, reservations, seats, airports, airplanes, meals, and so on. Thinking this way also helps prepare you for that terrifying moment your path diverges from the herd. Innovation is a powerful mass and a powerful mess.

Yes, innovation is more difficult than copying a solution or producing a single invention or two, but your competition won't be able to easily copy you either. Yes, there is no telling how long the process will take, but exploration is more exciting than tourism. Yes, there is no guarantee of success, but that makes victory all the better. Yes, you will be under pressure to grow to satisfy the new market you create, but you can have that market to yourself. Yes, you will have to keep your price low, but you can keep competitors away for decades.

Get comfortable with discomfort and keep going.

The Mythical Expert

Another feeling that accompanies entrepreneurship, at least in my case, is the feeling of being totally unprepared for the task at hand. Closely related to our urge to copy is our reverence for expertise. An expert, after all, is simply someone we aspire to copy. But experts only live in the walled city, for expertise only exists for the known. The king may bestow a title, but you're still going to die at the award ceremony if you have to pee.[107] Outside the wall there are no experts, just survivors and bones.

If your goal is to incrementally improve an existing business, then expertise in that area of business is certainly valuable. Incremental improvements are far less likely to fail than audacious innovation. And expertise is fundable: I am more likely to invest in your company if you have years of experience doing what you plan to do again. But what if you aren't going to copy? Can you even be an expert?

Does being a lawyer qualify you to run an airline? Does being a glassblower or massage therapist qualify you to run a payment company? Does being a produce vendor qualify you to run a bank? Does being seventeen qualify you to do anything?[108] Can you imagine a CEO saying, "We want to build the world's largest bank, so have HR arrange a dozen interviews with people who sell lettuce"?

---

[107] Tycho Brahe, the famous astronomer, died from a burst bladder because he could not leave a banquet before the king.
[108] Kamprad was so young when he started IKEA that he needed an adult's signature on the registration forms.

I often meet people who want to build something new but feel they lack sufficient expertise. Their assertion is correct, but not complete. The same lack of expertise applies to everyone on the planet. Once you realize that the world's greatest innovators were people who, just like you, had no formal qualifications to do what they did, your universe of perfect problems blossoms. Innovation has no experts.

The problem with worshipping expertise is the silent excuse that follows the phrase, *If I only knew more about . . .* People don't even bother uttering the heartbreaking second part, lest they hear themselves say: *. . . and therefore I shouldn't try.* I want people to say instead: *. . . but I will after I succeed.*

Do you feel unqualified to be an entrepreneur? Join the club. Qualification comes only from successful experience, and successful experience by definition cannot exist in the case of an unsolved problem. Qualification matters only in the world of copying, not in the world of entrepreneurship. If you are waiting for qualification, you can only ever be qualified to do something that has already been done.

But if expertise is not a prerequisite for entrepreneurship, is there any quality that matters? Do entrepreneurs possess some special trait that allows them to thrive outside the wall? If one were stubborn enough, could this trait possibly be learned?

Stubbornness

Among all the entrepreneurs I studied, perseverance, often displayed as stubbornness, seemed to be the most common trait.

Giannini once said, "There are only three kinds of politicians: those who can be persuaded, those who can be intimidated, and those who can be bought."[109] If you were in Giannini's way, he would befriend you, bully you, or buy you, *but you were getting out of his way.*

Though too modest during our interview to admit what a great fighter he was, Herb Kelleher certainly shared Giannini's grit. As evidence, one need only look to 1969 when Southwest was out of money and hopelessly ensnarled in the courts. Herb said to the board of directors, "Gentlemen, let's go one more round with them. I will continue to represent the company in court, and I'll postpone any legal fees and pay every cent of the court costs out of my own pocket."[110] Herb then dispensed such a legal smackdown that the local papers recommended people attend court simply for the entertainment value.

Entrepreneurial stubbornness is dynamic. One can be stubborn in refusal to change, but one can also be stubborn in action. It is more than just thinking you are right, it is a compulsion to move forward. But what supplies this energy? The answer brings us back to how it all begins: a perfect problem. Something you care deeply about.

The Perfect Problem

If you choose to leave the city, or for whatever reason find yourself outside its walls, what will keep you going? Will you be able

---

[109] *The Saturday Evening Post,* December 4, 1947, p. 131.
[110] Kevin Freiberg and Jackie Freiberg. *Nuts!: Southwest Airlines' Crazy Recipe for Business and Personal Success* (New York: Crown, 1998), pp. 17–18.

to ignore all the signs telling you to quit? Is there something that you truly care about? It probably isn't money or fame.

Money and fame are weak motivators. We tend to over-value both commodities because they are easy to measure. The view looks better from the outside than it does from within. The scales go to infinity but with diminishing and sometimes negative returns. You can actually be too rich and too famous, but don't complain about it to those of us who made you so.

A. P. Giannini was rich enough to retire at thirty-one, but he started a bank to help "the little fellow." Here was a fatherless son of immigrants who wanted to help the people he knew so well. We can only guess at his reason, but it certainly wasn't money. My guess is that he saw some problem he wanted to fix.

Problems are beautiful things, especially when it comes to motivation. If you care about a problem deeply enough, for whatever reason, your motivation can be infinite. Problems are as clear as seeing a friend sleeping in his car. No expert has to tell you that something is a problem, you just know. A real problem is obvious.

Problems are also plentiful. Anyone looking for a good idea to start a business need look no further than whatever upset them in the last month. For example, it truly bothered me that I lost that glass sale. It truly bothered me that I felt ripped off by the credit card companies. It truly bothered me that I couldn't understand my monthly statements or why they were taking my money for random reasons.

You don't simply choose the problem, the problem must also choose you. In other words, don't pick some problem that you think other people might have, pick a problem you know *you* have. When I find the right problem, I no longer feel anger, I feel energy.

For instance, I care more about the elderly than I do about the young. Now, I can think of several logical reasons why helping someone who is going to live for decades instead of months is a better use of my efforts. But for some reason, I'm motivated to help old people. I'm a better volunteer at the nursing home than the day-care center. Anger and attraction are emotions where we cannot choose our subject.

There is also something magical about solving a problem that you care about. The reward is internal. Nobody has to tell you "good job" or put your name on the bank door. You know it. Even if you are the only person who knows what you have done, your satisfaction is undiminished. In fact, solving a problem I care about may give me so much joy that I don't even want to explain it to anyone else, they just wouldn't understand.

CHAPTER 18

Back to Zero

SUDDENLY we won. At the time of our victory we had no idea how Square beat Amazon, but as I type these words five years later, the pattern is clear. We know what it is like to become obsessed with a problem nobody has solved. We understand why the urge to copy is so strong. We know the differences between entrepreneurship and business, and we see Innovation Stacks everywhere. We know how it feels outside the wall.

We also understand the two main reasons people overlook this pattern. First, entrepreneurship is rare: most of the things in our lives are copies of copies. Second, even if we discover something truly new, we lack the words to describe our findings. *Entrepreneurship* these days just means business.

So what? After completing this book, I had research, results, data, and details, not to mention a pack of Herb's smokes. But one question still gnawed away at me: *Did this knowledge help?* Can understanding a powerful phenome-non help you harness that power?

Before I could determine if this new knowledge was valuable, however, I had to control for a few other variables that had also recently changed. After Square's IPO, life got weird.

Hot Air

On November 19, 2015, Square listed its stock on the NYSE, and I was suddenly taller and more interesting than I had ever been. This newfound popularity extended to people I had never dreamed of meeting—including movie stars, MVPs, and even a group of clandestine campers. If you are a conspiracy theorist you will be happy to know that, yes, there are secret societies of powerful people that meet in the woods. I was personally escorted to one of these events by the relative of a US President. I would say more, but these people take their privacy seriously. And I take their serious-ness seriously.

Camouflage oxfords notwithstanding, I suddenly had money and access to a world that I never even knew existed. I thought that having money, experience, and access to power-ful people would make solving future problems easier. Not so much.

It's like food: hunger is terrible, but that doesn't mean the opposite extreme is the goal. I learned this lesson liter-ally. Twice after Square's IPO I received invitations to dine in restaurants that were so fancy one of the dinner courses was air.[111] Just *air*. Ironically, both restaurants were in San Francisco, where the air often smells like a drunk rugby team trying to extinguish a burning bale of marijuana.

Money, experience, and access are great if you want to enter an established business. The money allows you to hire a team of the most talented people from that industry and give them whatever tools they require. Experience prevents you from making the mistakes that everyone knows can doom your efforts. Access allows your ideas to find the people who count. But if you are building something truly new, these things barely matter.

Michael Jordan, arguably the best basketball player in history, decided to switch to baseball at the height of his career. He could afford the best of everything, from trainers to tour buses. He had amazing athletic abilities and a legendary work ethic. But none of this stopped him from chasing curve balls into the dirt for a year before returning to re-dominate the NBA. It doesn't matter if you arrive on a fancy bus wearing your own brand of shoes and can dunk from the free throw line; that stuff doesn't help your bat hit the ball.

Having piles of money and contacts is only useful for a game people already know how to play. When it comes to doing something new, we are all even. Entrepreneurship starts at zero. One thing that differentiates entrepreneurs

---

[111] The waiter presented a mysterious dessert concealed by smoke under glass. In one disdainful flourish he lifted the cloche to reveal that the smoke *was* the dessert. Cough.

from the rest of us is their willingness to start. How comforting to know that we all start in the same place.

Square One

After I was done with the daily management of Square, my family moved back to St. Louis. I returned to my glass studio and began rehabbing some old buildings. The manual work calmed my heart and calloused my hands. It was a welcome change from the payments industry, which had calmed my hands but calloused my heart.

One morning, my coworker Anatoly arrived trembling and pointing to his phone. We spoke different languages, but the pictures were horrifyingly clear. His son Daniil had been shot while delivering a pizza the night before in a sketchy part of town. He was barely alive in a local hospital and his poor father was so lost that he actually came into work, not that we did any. We just sat crying together on five-gallon buckets of drywall compound until it was clear that there was nothing we could do. Daniil Maksimenko died that evening.

I spent the next year in depressed denial—the city I know doesn't kill kids. But it did. I was trying to understand something that defied logic: why would anyone shoot a pizza delivery kid while he was still in his car? Unable to make sense of this tragedy, I eventually concluded that the assailants were just mentally ill.

But my explanation used bad math. There were three assailants, any one of whom could have stopped the assault.

So what are the odds of a person being shoot-a-stranger-in-the-head sick? Probably less than 1/1000, but let's be conservative and go with that number. Since there were three assailants, and they would each have to be afflicted, we have to cube the odds $(1/1000)^3 = 1/1,000,000,000$. My "they were mentally ill" explanation had a one in a billion chance of being correct. This forced me to an even worse conclusion: there are parts of my city where shooting a stranger in the head is somehow normal. This new conclusion just deepened my depression. I could only distract myself for a day or two before the smell of fresh drywall or pepperoni would choke me up. Finally, in desperation, I went to the site of the murder.

I don't claim to know what the boys who shot Daniil were thinking, but having now spent some time in their neighborhood, I can see why they might have that attitude. The schools are terrible, the streets are deadly, and there are few paths out. If you don't have the right education, most doors are closed. It took me another year to find a door we could pry open.

St. Louis needed programmers. Jack and I had closed Square's original St. Louis office because we couldn't hire enough coders. Programming is a funny profession: the best coders are self-taught, and formal credentials are only marginally valuable. I knew from having hired hundreds of coders that about 30 percent of the population has brains and personalities that predispose them to become successful programmers. I ran the numbers.

More than 100,000 people lived below the poverty line

in St. Louis, so more than 30,000 poor people had the potential to get well-paying jobs as programmers. Even if we could only reach 10 percent of that group *who already had the natural talent*, it would be a good start. I also knew that a fresh supply of programmers would help all the companies in St. Louis grow. I founded LaunchCode.org to address both problems: a lack of talent for businesses and a lack of opportunity for people.

Leaving Another Walled City

The critical moment when you become an entrepreneur is when you realize that you cannot copy the solution. At this point, you must either create something new or live with the problem. Since the programmer shortage was worldwide, I had hoped that someone had a solution that Launch-Code could copy. All I found were educational programs, but they were expensive and many of their graduates failed to get programming jobs. I soon learned why.

The programming market, not surprisingly, had simply copied what worked for other industries: namely education, which works for most labor shortages. If we have a shortage of welders, then demand for their skills increases wages. Attracted by the money, people train to become welders and get jobs until the market balances. For some reason, however, simply copying this educational solution didn't work for programming, as evidenced by the fact that the coder shortage increased annually despite skyrocketing salaries. I had to learn why we could not copy the solution.

Programming is not like welding or most other professions because coders can do "negative work." If Pat is a bad welder, her welds may fail, but that's the extent of the damage. She cannot be so bad that she makes her coworkers' welds disintegrate. Coding is different. If Pat is a terrible programmer, she can be more destructive than a monkey with a machine gun. One malformed query can corrupt a whole database. And who makes most of these mistakes? Newbies.

For this very logical reason, most businesses won't hire programmers with fewer than two years' experience. No experience, no job. Therefore: no job, no experience. In St. Louis, so many companies refused to hire new coders that the whole job market locked up. The few companies that risked hiring newbies were actually penalized by the market. They faced extra training and supervision costs only to have a majority of their new hires quit after two years. This makes sense because if you are only able to get a job at one firm, the odds are low that you actually want to work there. You may take the job, but only until you have enough experience to leave. The market for employing coders was broken.

Meanwhile, training was also a toxic mess. High wages created a cluster of coding camps that sprang up like mushrooms after a long rain. And like mushrooms, it was hard to differentiate the safe from the poisonous. Hopeful people borrowed money to attend these boot camps only to learn worthless skills. Accredited institutions were no better. Teacher salaries were half what industry paid, encouraging "those who couldn't"[112] to teach. Even good instructors faced a market where programming trends changed every six months, so the curriculum quickly became obsolete. The market for training coders was broken.

But I not only had this new perfect problem, I also had the research for this book, a bunch of money, contacts, and the GPS coordinates of a heavily wooded area. So, how much did it help?

The money and contacts were of marginal value. LaunchCode began with $20,000. The project has been self-supporting since that initial investment. This is not to say that we don't raise funds; just that my money didn't matter because even without it there were plenty of other funding sources. More importantly, the problems we did have could not be solved with money.

My contacts were also not much help. Hundreds of people have given their time to make LaunchCode succeed, but they were drawn by the mission and our results. Democrats and Republicans have helped us, but not because of me or my experience with Square. President Obama's office called us one day to say that they loved our program and that the President would like to meet some of our graduates. He sang their praises in a speech,[113] but afterward his only words to me were, *"Who are you?"*

---

[112] "Those who can, do. Those who can't, teach. Those who can't teach, teach gym."—George Bernard Shaw & Woody Allen

[113] Remarks by President Obama at the National League of Cities Conference, March 09, 2015, https://www.c-span.org/video/?c4530694/user-clip-obama-talks-lashanas-success-launchcode.

The big challenge with LaunchCode was not money or contacts, but that nobody had ever solved these issues of the tech shortage and lack of opportunity simultaneously (or separately, for that matter). I knew the existing system had failed for decades; otherwise there would be no programmer shortage or frustrated people murdering pizza delivery drivers. What I didn't know at first was how to solve either the education or placement problem. But I now understood how innovation evolves, and this knowledge was a huge help.

We knew we couldn't copy the existing system, so instead of beginning with education we began with job placement. Once we figured out how to get our coders jobs, we quickly ran out of coders, so we knew we had to begin training new talent. But traditional education was too slow and expensive, so we knew we had to train differently. Harvard had a great online course, but it had only a 1 percent completion rate, so we knew we had to find a way to help the students finish the course. We discovered how to boost the completion rate to over 50 percent, but that raised our costs from $100 per person to $1000 per person. We were tempted to begin charging tuition, but we knew how price impacts entrepreneurial companies, so we had to keep our price free. And so on.

It's not a magic cure, as LaunchCode has only gotten jobs for a few thousand people so far. We are still searching for the innovation that will expand that number to millions. LaunchCode's specific Innovation Stack is not the point. The point is that *understanding* Innovation Stacks made us less hesitant to act. Even if you have just spent three years researching and writing a book on entrepreneurship, the journey is still scary. Your buddies, bodies, and brains scream at you to return to the herd.

But we knew the pattern: find a problem and learn how others have solved it. If nobody has, try something different even though this will feel weird. When your new solution creates new problems, repeat the process. Copy what you can, but invent when necessary. And keep going until you finally have a solution, knowing that the accolades will arrive only after they are irrelevant. Our knowledge of the Innovation Stack helped us *move*. And movement is the key.

Going Small

Please don't be dissuaded because the four companies I've profiled in this book are billion-dollar behemoths. The process works just as well for smaller problems, and it's actually easier. If a single invention or two solves the problem, congratulations. Innovation Stacks with a dozen or more elements may provide a market-dominating position, but don't invent for invention's sake. Simple solutions are beautiful.

For instance, my friend Greg invented a new solution when his son threw a fit in a mall. The child wanted something and when his parents refused, he proceeded to throw a public tantrum. Ever the entrepreneur, Greg got to work with the resources he had: he hastily assembled all the gawkers into a formal Tantrum Rating Committee. When the kid took a breath, each audience member was invited to provide critique and suggestions on how the tantrum could be improved, while the boy lay face-down and mortified on the mall's peach composite flooring. The result was a swift resolution of the problem and a young man who vastly prefers online shopping.

Even if you have a more traditional business, a bit of entrepreneurship can give you a competitive advantage. Another friend of mine runs a construction company, but with a twist. He has developed an Innovation Stack that allows him to successfully employ ex-offenders. Employing people who have recently left prison is notoriously challenging, so he had to rework how work works. The five elements in his Stack allow him to have a more stable and productive workforce. In an industry famous for labor shortages, he hammers the competition.

I chose big examples for this book because the companies are familiar and demonstrate the power of Innovation Stacks. The same power that allows a produce vendor to build the world's biggest bank or a teenager to assemble the world's biggest furniture store is available to us all. As we have seen, even great entrepreneurs don't invent just to invent. If a small Innovation Stack solves your problem, well, problem solved.

You Can't Unread This

Reading this book will make you no more an expert than I became writing it. There are no experts of the new. We all begin with nothing except a problem that nobody else has solved. We can't even discuss it with our friends because there are no words for what we do, just a vocabulary built for relentless replication. But there is a powerful process that helps you.

And you now see the process! You understand that while entrepreneurship is rare, the skills of the entrepreneur are something we all possess. The entrepreneur takes that first step. In fact, my original title of this book was *First Steps off a Flat Earth*.

I hope this book helps you or someone you know take that first step and many more. Perhaps you will see something wrong and instead of just accepting it you will try something new. I hope you have gained a bit of confidence, angst, or understanding. Whatever gets you going.

But now that you have read this book you have lost something as well. You can no longer look at a problem and say, *"Nothing can be done."* You can't even say, *"I can't do it because I am lacking (fill in your excuse du jour)."* You can only say either, *"I'm not going to do anything"* or *"I am going to solve this problem."* Because we have seen how world-changing entrepreneurs had few if any qualifications when they began their journeys. Knowing what you now know about entrepreneurship prevents you from dismissing a problem as unsolvable.

We have so many problems in the world, and some of them may be perfect for you. Maybe you will find one that a million other people share, but can find no expert to solve. Maybe you will become that expert, not by copying but by creating something new. Maybe you will make our world a little better.

Find a problem you care about, one that will drive you

even when there is no other positive feedback. See if others have solved similar problems in ways you can copy, but know that you also have another option. For now you know how innovation appears and how it evolves. You know the qualifications for true entrepreneurship, and the rewards for success. Go make it right. Square up.

Acknowledgments

I'VE NEVER DONE anything significant alone. I've also never done anything well the first time, including this book, which is now on its seventh rewrite.

The first draft of the manuscript came from material Jeff Alexander and Dan Josefson helped me piece together from hours and hours of my recordings. Though only a few paragraphs survived the next six drafts, they gave me the start I needed.

I then got my friend Amy Scharff involved as my editor and collaborator through the final five rewrites. Both Amy and I learned our writing craft at Ladue's public high school in St. Louis, which had an English department better than most liberal arts colleges. Amy, your writing and honest feedback were critical to making this book what it is.

Doug Auer, John Berglund, Jack Dorsey, Achilles Karakas, Joe Maxwell, Jeff Mazur, Matthew Porter and Greg Rogers: thank you for leading the organizations we started. Without your daily efforts, I could not begin anything new. You have my deepest respect for what you do.

My parents, James and Edith McKelvey, raised me to believe that anything is possible without once giving me unsolicited advice. Judy McKelvey, who joined our family after Mom died, is also one of my role models for what is possible.

Herb Kelleher. You were generous with your time, and I wish you had had more of it. I miss you.

Jim Levine, book agent to some of my idols, not only helped me sell the manuscript, he helped me structure it. Rewrites five through seven have been under Jim's uplifted eyebrow.

Trevor Goring drew a great graphic novel of A. P. Giannini's story, even though it was completely removed. More show, less tell.

Jim Keller, rock-star chip architect, gave me candid feedback when everyone else thought it was good enough. It wasn't; hopefully now it is.

Kaushik Viswanath, Trish Daly, and Adrian Zackheim from Portfolio made this a polished work. Speaking as someone who used to own a book printing company, professionals like you are the reason I will never self-publish.

Anna, Jimmy, and Margaret. Thanks for always making me feel at home wherever we are on the planet.

Index

....

Note: Page numbers in *italics* indicate photographs and illustrations.

INDEX

INDEX

INDEX